PARABLES
WORKBOOK

PARABLES WORKBOOK

THE MYSTERIES OF GOD'S KINGDOM REVEALED THROUGH THE STORIES JESUS TOLD

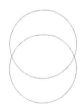

JOHN MACARTHUR

WITH KAREN LEE-THORP

HarperChristian Resources

Parables Workbook
Copyright © 2016 by John MacArthur

Requests for information should be addressed to:
HarperChristian Resources, 3900 Sparks Dr. SE, Grand Rapids, Michigan 49546

ISBN 978-0-310-68642-2 (softcover)
ISBN 978-0-310-68643-9 (ebook)

CONTENTS

INTRODUCTION

Jesus' parables were ingeniously simple word pictures with profound spiritual lessons. His teaching was full of everyday stories. Some of them were no more than fleeting remarks about commonplace incidents, objects, or persons. In fact, the most compact of all Jesus' short stories does not even fill a complete verse of Scripture. Jesus was the master storyteller, and there was not a truism so familiar or doctrine so complex that He could not give it new depth and insight through the telling of a simple story. These narratives epitomize the simple yet powerful profundity of His message and teaching style.

While the parables illustrate and clarify truth for those with "ears to hear"—a phrase Jesus often repeats in His narratives—they have the opposite effect on those who oppose and reject Christ. The symbolism hides the truth from anyone without the discipline or desire to seek out Christ's meaning. This is one of the reasons why Jesus adopted this style of teaching. It was a divine judgment against those who met His teaching with scorn, unbelief, or apathy.

Yet the parables don't just reflect God's judgment; they also show His mercy. Like any good illustration, Jesus' parables naturally aroused interest and attention in the minds of those who were not necessarily hard-set against the truth but simply lacked aptitude of spiritual matters or had no taste for hearing doctrine expounded in more dogmatic language. No doubt the parables had the effect of awakening the minds of many such people who were struck by the simplicity of Jesus' stories and became eager to discover the underlying meanings. For others—including, surely, some whose first exposure to the truth provoked skepticism, indifference, or even rejection—the graphic imagery of the parables helped keep truth rooted in their memories until it sprang forth in faith and understanding.

In short, Jesus' parables had a twofold purpose. On the one hand, they hid the truth from those self-righteous or self-satisfied people who had no discipline or desire to seek out Christ's true meaning. On the other hand, they revealed truth to those eager souls with childlike faith who were hungering and thirsting for righteousness. Jesus thanked His Father for both results: "I thank You, Father, Lord of heaven and earth, that You have hidden these things from the wise and prudent and have revealed them to babes. Even so, Father, for so it seemed good in Your sight" (Matthew 11:25–26).

Before looking at specific parables, it would be good to consider the genre. What is a parable, and how does it differ from other illustrative forms—metaphors, similes, fables, allegories, and the like? A parable is not merely a simple analogy. It's an elongated simile or metaphor with a distinctly spiritual lesson contained in the analogy. Short figures of speech like "as strong as a horse" or "as quick as a rabbit" are plain similes—simple and straightforward enough not to require an explanation. A parable extends the comparison into a longer story or more complex metaphor, and the meaning (always a point of spiritual truth) is not necessarily obvious. Most of Jesus' parables demanded some kind of explanation. The important component of every parable is the central lesson. In cases where the symbolism is complex (such as the parable of the soils), Jesus almost always explains the symbolism.

In this study, we will look at the context that motivated Jesus to teach in parables and then take a tour of twenty-one parables in the Gospels to see what they teach. ✳

THE PARABLES OF JESUS

	Parable	Matthew	Mark	Luke
1.	Lamp Under a Basket	5:14–16	4:21–22	8:16–17 11:33–36
2.	A Wise Man Builds on Rock and a Foolish Man Builds on Sand	7:24–27		6:47–49
3.	Unshrunk (New) Cloth on an Old Garment	9:16	2:21	5:36
4.	New Wine in Old Wineskins	9:17	2:22	5:37–38
5.	The Sower	13:3–23	4:2–20	8:4–15
6.	The Tares (Weeds)	13:24–30		
7.	The Mustard Seed	13:31–32	4:30–32	13:18–19
8.	The Leaven	13:33		13:20–21
9.	The Hidden Treasure	13:44		
10.	The Pearl of Great Price	13:45–46		
11.	The Dragnet	13:47–50		
12.	The Lost Sheep	18:12–14		15:3–7
13.	The Unforgiving Servant	18:23–35		
14.	The Workers in the Vineyard	20:1–16		
15.	The Two Sons	21:28–32		
16.	The Wicked Vinedressers	21:33–45	12:1–12	20:9–19
17.	The Wedding Feast	22:2–14		
18.	The Fig Tree	24:32–44	13:28–32	21:29–33
19.	The Wise and Foolish Virgins	25:1–13		
20.	The Talents	25:14–30		
21.	The Growing Seed		4:26–29	
22.	The Absent Householder		13:33–37	
23.	The Creditor and Two Debtors			7:41–43
24.	The Good Samaritan			10:30–37
25.	A Friend in Need			11:5–13
26.	The Rich Fool			12:16–21
27.	The Watchful Servants			12:35–40
28.	The Faithful Servant and the Evil Servant			12:42–48
29.	The Barren Fig Tree			13:6–9
30.	The Great Supper			14:16–24
31.	Building a Tower and a King Making War			14:25–35
32.	The Lost Coin			15:8–10
33.	The Lost Son			15:11–32
34.	The Unjust Steward			16:1–13
35.	The Rich Man and Lazarus			16:19–31
36.	Unprofitable Servants			17:7–10
37.	The Persistent Widow			18:1–8
38.	The Pharisee and the Tax Collector			18:9–14
39.	The Minas (Pounds)			19:11–27

Source: *The MacArthur Study Bible* (Nashville, TN: Thomas Nelson, 1993), page 1417.

HOW TO USE THIS WORKBOOK

This workbook is designed as a companion to *Parables: The Mysteries of God's Kingdom Revealed Through the Stories Jesus Told*. It will serve as a directed Bible study to help you explore many of the parables that Jesus gave to His followers and the main lessons and principles that Christ was trying to teach. You are encouraged to cross-check the Scriptures used in the workbook and grapple with the passages on which the main teachings are based.

Note that each of the lessons in this workbook correspond with the chapter of the same name in *Parables*. The one exception is the bonus lesson at the end of the study, which is based on the parable of the lost son and corresponds to material found in *The Prodigal Son: An Astonishing Study of the Parable Jesus Told to Unveil God's Grace for You*.

You may choose to use this workbook for individual study or small-group study. Each of the lessons has been designed to help you meditate on the parables of Jesus and hear them not just as stories spoken long ago but as words said to us today. The goal is to help your heart hear and respond to what your mind reads—and then apply what you discover to your everyday life.

Each lesson begins with an **overview** of the main objectives and the chapters in the *Parables* book that you should **read**. You will then be given three quotes from the book with questions to help you **review** the content and start thinking about the theme of the lesson. Write your thoughts on the lines provided, and if you need more space, use a separate notebook. If you are planning on using this in a small-group setting, keep in mind you will get more out of the discussion if you take time to prepare and work through the exercises prior to your meeting.

In the next section, you will **make the connection** by exploring one or two Scripture passages connected to the main theme of the lesson. You will not only analyze the parable and the other Scripture passage being presented but also be challenged to reconsider any thoughts or attitudes you have that might be inconsistent with the Bible. Following this, you will **explore the key points** of the lesson and draw some conclusions about how the parables you just examined relate to your day-to-day life. And finally, there will be a couple of questions about **living the parable** that invites you to pull together what you have studied and identify the primary insight you want to integrate into your life in a practical way.

The closing section of each lesson will provide you with a way to continue to **reflect and respond** on the study's theme. In this section you will find suggested Scripture readings for spending time alone with God during five days of the coming week. Each daily reading will include prompts for reflection, response, and prayer.

If you are planning to use this workbook for a group study, you are encouraged to make certain each member of the group has a personal copy of both the book and the workbook. At the back of this workbook you will find notes and information to assist you if you are planning on leading a small group through this study. ✳

One Ominous Day in Galilee

Then one was brought to [Jesus] who was demon-possessed, blind and mute; and He healed him, so that the blind and mute man both spoke and saw. And all the multitudes were amazed and said, "Could this be the Son of David?" Now when the Pharisees heard it they said, "This fellow does not cast out demons except by Beelzebub, the ruler of the demons."

MATTHEW 12:22–24

Main Objectives

In this study, you will (1) look at why Jesus shifted from teaching straightforward sermons to teaching in parables, (2) examine what role the Sabbath has played in the history of redemption, and (3) consider what our words and actions say about our attitude toward Jesus.

Read and Review

Read the introduction and chapter 1 from *Parables* and answer the questions that follow. If you're meeting in a small group, you might want to have someone read each of the following excerpts from *Parables* aloud before you discuss the questions related to it.

A Shift in Style

One very busy day near the end of Jesus' second year of public ministry, He had an encounter with some hostile Pharisees, and the whole character of His teaching

Jesus' parables were ingeniously simple **word pictures** with profound **spiritual lessons.** (*Parables*, page xiii)

suddenly changed. He no longer preached straightforward sermons peppered with key prophetic texts from the Old Testament. From that point on, whenever He taught publicly, He spoke in parables. Such an abrupt shift in Jesus' teaching style was a portent of judgment against the religious elite of Israel and all who followed their lead. (*Parables*, page 1)

You have heard that it was said. . . . But I say to you . . . (Matthew 5:21–22, 27–28)

1. Read Matthew 5:21–30. How would you describe Jesus' style of teaching in this passage?

_____

_____

_____

_____

_____

When He had opened the book, He found the place where it was written . . . (Luke 4:17)

2. Read Luke 4:16–27. How would you describe Jesus' style of teaching in this passage? How is it like or unlike the way he teaches in Matthew 5:21–30?

_____

_____

_____

_____

_____

Another parable He put forth to them . . . (Matthew 13:31)

3. Read Matthew 13:31–35. How would you describe Jesus' style of teaching in this passage? How is His teaching in parables like or unlike the way he teaches in Matthew 5:21–30 and Luke 4:16–27?

_____

_____

_____

_____

_____

_____

The Pharisees and the Sabbath

Matthew 12 begins with a major confrontation provoked by a Pharisaical Sabbath-enforcement squad. The disciples were hungry and had plucked some heads of grain to eat while walking through a field of wheat or barley on the Sabbath. The Pharisees were up in arms and contended with Jesus over the propriety of what His disciples had done (Matthew 12:1–2). According to the Pharisees' rules, even casually plucking a handful of grain was a form of gleaning, and therefore it was work. This was precisely the kind of seemingly inconsequential act that the Pharisees routinely targeted, turning even the bare necessities of life into a thousand unwritten Sabbatarian taboos. . . .

People lived in **fear** that if they accidentally violated or neglected some trivial **Sabbath rule**, the Pharisees would call them on the carpet and threaten them with **excommunication** or, in the worst cases, **stoning.** (*Parables*, page 5)

Jesus replied by showing the folly of a rule that forbids an act of human necessity on a day set aside for the benefit of humanity: "The Sabbath was made for man, and not man for the Sabbath" (Mark 2:27). He rebuked the Pharisees for condemning the guiltless, and then added that famous declaration of His own divine authority: "The Son of Man is Lord even of the Sabbath" (Matthew 12:8). (Parables, page 5)

4. How is it different to think about the Sabbath as made for man, as opposed to man for the Sabbath? How would one's approach to the Sabbath be different?

_____

_____

_____

_____

_____

_____

5. Why is it a claim of divine authority to say, "The Son of Man is Lord even of the Sabbath"?

_____

_____

_____

_____

_____

_____

6. Which do you think is more of a problem among Christians today: needless legalism or too little regard for God's commands? Give an example.

_____

_____

_____

_____

The religious leaders' blind **hatred** was such that they frankly did not care whether [Jesus'] **messianic credentials** were legitimate or not; they were determined to **dissuade** people from following Him no matter what it took. (*Parables*, page 6)

Legalism: strict, literal, or excessive conformity to the law or to a religious or moral code. (*Merriam-Webster*)

The Unpardonable Sin

The hard-hearted intentionality of the Pharisees' sin is the main factor that made it unpardonable. Why would they credit Satan with what Jesus had done through the power of the Holy Spirit? They had just watched Him vanquish demons. They fully grasped who Jesus was and with what authority He spoke and acted (Luke 6:10–11; John 11:47–48; 12:9; Acts 4:16)—and yet they hated Him with a devilish hatred anyway. It's clear that they were lying when they said He was the devilish one. . . .

Why was their statement such a grievous offense against the Holy Spirit? For one thing, the demoniac's healing was as much a work of the Holy Spirit as it was a work of Christ. All Jesus' miracles were done according to the will of the Father through the power of the Holy Spirit (Luke 4:14; John 5:19, 30; 8:28; Acts 10:38). Therefore to attribute our Lord's miracles to Satan was to credit Satan with the Holy Spirit's work. Because they knew better, the Pharisees' abominable insult was a direct, deliberate, diabolical blasphemy against the Spirit of God. (Parables, pages 12–13)

Anyone who speaks a word against the Son of Man, it will be forgiven him; but whoever speaks against the Holy Spirit, it will not be forgiven him, either in this age or in the age to come. (Matthew 12:32)

The Pharisees . . . said, "This fellow does not cast out demons except by Beelzebub, the ruler of the demons."
(Matthew 12:24)

7. Why did the Pharisees' words in Matthew 12:24 constitute a blasphemy against the Holy Spirit?

_____

_____

_____

_____

_____

8. Do you think atheists today are guilty of blasphemy against the Holy Spirit? Why or why not?

_____

_____

_____

_____

_____

[Jesus'] **warning** about this one extraordinary act of unforgivable **blasphemy** was purposely prefaced by a comprehensive statement declaring **every other** imaginable kind of "sin and blasphemy" **forgivable.** (*Parables*, page 11)

9. What were the heart-level sins that led the Pharisees to lie about the miracles Jesus was performing instead of enthusiastically embracing them as coming from God?

_____

_____

_____

_____

_____

_____

Make the Connection

Read the following Scripture passages and answer the questions provided. If you are meeting in a small group, you might want to have someone read each passage aloud before you discuss the questions related to it.

Jewish **tradition** prohibited the practice of **medicine** on the Sabbath, except in life-threatening situations. But no actual Old Testament law **forbade** the giving of medicine, healing, or any other **acts of mercy** on the *Sabbath*. (*MacArthur Bible Commentary*, page 1145)

The Pharisees went out and plotted against Him, how they might destroy Him.

But when Jesus knew it, He withdrew from there. And great multitudes followed Him, and He healed them all. Yet He warned them not to make Him known, that it might be fulfilled which was spoken by Isaiah the prophet, saying:

"Behold! My Servant whom I have chosen,
My Beloved in whom My soul is well pleased!
I will put My Spirit upon Him,
And He will declare justice to the Gentiles.
He will not quarrel nor cry out,

Nor will anyone hear His voice in the streets.
A bruised reed He will not break,
And smoking flax He will not quench,
Till He sends forth justice to victory;
And in His name Gentiles will trust." (Matthew 12:14-21)

[Jesus] came not to gather the strong for a **revolution**, but to show **mercy** to the **weak.** (*MacArthur Bible Commentary*, page 1146)

10. Why did Jesus withdraw from the conflict with the Pharisees?

_____
_____
_____
_____
_____

After this, Jesus would peremptorily **conceal** the **truth** from [the Pharisees] by the use of **parables** in His public teaching. (*Parables*, page 13)

11. What does the passage from Isaiah that Matthew quotes tell us about Jesus and His ministry?

_____
_____
_____
_____
_____
_____
_____

12. How are these truths about Jesus still relevant to us today?

_____
_____
_____
_____
_____
_____

[Jesus said,] *"Either make the tree good and its fruit good, or else make the tree bad and its fruit bad; for a tree is known by its fruit. Brood of vipers! How can you, being evil, speak good things? For out of the abundance of the heart the mouth speaks. A good man out of the good treasure of his heart brings forth good things, and an evil man out of the evil treasure brings forth evil things. But I say to you that for every idle word men may speak, they will give account of it in the day of judgment. For by your words you will be justified, and by your words you will be condemned."* (Matthew 12:33–37)

Even a Pharisee such as Saul of Tarsus could be **forgiven** for speaking "against the Son of Man" or **persecuting** His followers, because his unbelief stemmed from **ignorance**. . . . But those who know His claims are true and **reject Him anyway** sin "against the Holy Spirit." (*MacArthur Bible Commentary*, page 1146)

13. According to Jesus, why was it inevitable the Pharisees would say ugly and lying things about Him?

_____
_____
_____
_____
_____
_____

But the fruit of the Spirit is love, joy, peace, long-suffering, kindness, goodness, faithfulness, gentleness, self-control. (Galatians 5:22–23)

14. What sort of fruit does a good tree produce? What are some examples of good fruit in a person's life?

_____

_____

_____

_____

_____

15. What do your words say about you? What is an example of something good they say about you, and what is an example of something you might need to work on?

_____

_____

_____

_____

_____

_____

Explore the Key Points

Take some time to consider how a few of the big ideas of this chapter intersect with your own life. It will be helpful to answer these questions on your own before you discuss them with your group. If you're meeting with a group, you may want to have someone read aloud the key point before you discuss it.

The Role of the Sabbath

In six days the LORD made the heavens and the earth, the sea, and all that is in them, and rested the seventh day. Therefore the LORD blessed the Sabbath day and hallowed it. (Exodus 20:11)

The Sabbath plays a key role in the history of redemption. On the seventh day of the week when God created the heavens and the earth, God rested from his work (see Genesis 2:1–3). He then declared the Sabbath holy as a gift to humanity (see Exodus 20:8–11). Because of humanity's sin, work is a never-ending drudgery, but God gave the Sabbath as an opportunity for humans to enter into the delight of the Lord's rest on a regular basis. It is a celebration of *the Lord's* finished work, and all humanity is urged to join the celebration.

But the full glory of the Sabbath was ultimately unveiled in the finished work of Christ (see John 19:30). This is why Paul declares in Colossians 2:16–17, "Let no one judge you in food or in drink, or regarding a festival or a new moon or sabbaths, which are a shadow of things to come, but the substance is of Christ." Christians already enjoy the rest of God's finished work in their lives, so formal Sabbath-keeping is no longer a *law* for Christians to observe. Rest is still good, but a formal keeping of the seventh day of the week is no longer binding on Christians.

[Jesus] said, "It is finished!" And bowing His head, He gave up His spirit. (John 19:30)

16. What purposes did the Sabbath have in the lives of the Jews before Jesus' coming? What did the Sabbath teach them and do for them if they kept it as it was intended?

_____

_____

_____

_____

Six days shall work be done, but the seventh day is a Sabbath of solemn rest, a holy convocation. (Leviticus 23:3)

17. Even though the Sabbath law is no longer binding on Christians, it is still good for us to have a rhythm of work and rest. What role does work play in your life? To what extent would you describe it as drudgery? Does it have any positive aspects?

_____

_____

_____

_____

18. What role does regular rest play in your life? What do you think a good rhythm of work and rest would look like for you?

_____

_____

_____

_____

There remains therefore a rest for the people of God. (Hebrews 4:9)

Forgivable Sin

In discussing the Pharisees' uniquely unforgivable blasphemy, Jesus made a comprehensive statement about every other imaginable kind of sin: "Therefore I say to you, every sin and blasphemy will be forgiven men" (Matthew 12:31). Note that Jesus was not saying that anyone's sin is forgiven *automatically* even if they don't repent and believe in Him. Every sin is bad enough to deserve eternal punishment as long as the sinner remains impenitent and unbelieving. "He who does not believe is condemned already, because he has not believed in the name of the only begotten Son of God" (John 3:18).

However, even the worst sin is forgivable—and complete forgiveness is guaranteed to every sinner who renounces his love of sin and turns to Christ as Savior. "If we *confess* our sins, He is faithful and just to forgive us our sins and to cleanse us from all unrighteousness" (1 John 1:9, emphasis added). In other words, when we agree with God concerning our own guilt, the atoning blood of Christ cleanses us from every kind of sin or blasphemy—no matter how abominable. Jesus Himself made this promise: "Most assuredly, I say to you, he who hears My word and believes in

[To "believe in the name"] includes **trust** and **commitment** to Christ as Lord and Savior, which results in receiving a **new nature**, which produces a **change** in heart and **obedience** to the Lord. (*MacArthur Bible Commentary*, page 1359)

Him who sent Me has everlasting life, and shall not come into judgment, but has passed from death into life" (John 5:24).

For all have sinned and fall short of the glory of God. (Romans 3:23)

19. Why do we deserve eternal punishment even if we have never committed any of the abominable sins of deliberate harm to other people?

_____

_____

_____

_____

"Vengeance is Mine, I will repay," says the Lord. (Romans 12:19)

20. Are there any sins that you can't imagine God forgiving—that you don't *want* Him to forgive? Child abuse? Rape? Mass murder? Explain your attitude.

_____

_____

_____

_____

Even the **vilest** sin is *forgivable*—and complete forgiveness is **guaranteed** to every sinner who **renounces** his love of sin and turns to Christ. (*Parables*, page 11)

21. Are there any sins you have committed that you have difficulty accepting forgiveness for? You don't have to name them to others, but do name them to yourself. God wants you to experience the complete freedom that comes from acknowledging your guilt there and believing Him when He says He forgives you.

_____

_____

_____

_____

Living the Parable

We've covered a lot in this lesson. Now it is your chance to pull it all together and decide what is the most important principle(s) you need to take to heart. You probably can't change your life in half a dozen ways this week, so prayerfully consider what is God's top priority for you.

22. What is your main takeaway(s) from this lesson? What do you want to take to heart as you go forward?

_____

_____

_____

_____

23. What are some things you will do to apply what you've learned?

_____

_____

_____

_____

_____

Reflect and Respond

At the end of each lesson, you will find suggested Scripture readings for spending time alone with God during five days of the coming week. Each day of this week's readings will deal with the theme of being teachable, as that was a key quality that the Pharisees lacked in their interactions with Jesus. Read each passage slowly, pausing to think about what is being said. Rather than approaching this as an assignment to complete, think of it as an encounter with your heavenly Father. Use any of the questions that are helpful.

Teachable: Able and willing to learn: capable of being taught. (*Merriam-Webster*)

Day 1

1. Read Psalm 32:8–9. What can we learn about teachability from the example of the horse and mule?

_____

_____

_____

_____

_____

Do not be like the horse or like the mule, which have no understanding. (Psalm 32:9)

2. Do you think of yourself as teachable? What is the evidence for or against?

_____

_____

_____

_____

_____

3. What do you think God means in verse 8 when He speaks of guiding us with His eye? How does that work in practice?

_____

_____

_____

_____

_____

I will instruct you and teach you in the way you should go; I will guide you with My eye. (Psalm 32:8)

4. How is that different from being led around by a bit and bridle?

_____

_____

_____

_____

_____

Blessed is he whose transgression is forgiven, whose sin is covered.
(Psalm 32:1)

5. The context for this passage has to do with repentance. Read Psalm 32:1–5. How do confession and repentance put us in the right frame of mind to be teachable?

_____

_____

_____

_____

_____

_____

Day 2

Let him show by good conduct that his works are done in the meekness of wisdom.
(James 3:13)

1. Read James 3:13–18. What is "the meekness of wisdom" (verse 13)? What would be an example of wise meekness?

_____

_____

_____

_____

_____

If you have bitter envy and self-seeking in your hearts, do not boast and lie against the truth.
(James 3:14)

2. How do envy and self-seeking (see verse 14) get in the way of attaining wisdom?

_____

_____

_____

_____

_____

The wisdom that is from above is first pure, then peaceable, gentle, willing to yield, full of mercy and good fruits. (James 3:17)

3. What are the qualities of someone who is wise enough to be teachable (see verse 17)?

_____

_____

_____

_____

_____

_____

4. Which one of these qualities would you like to develop more of in your life? Why?

_____
_____
_____
_____
_____

5. How do you think that quality would make you more open to learning from God?

_____
_____
_____
_____
_____
_____

Day 3

1. Read 2 Timothy 2:14–16. What does it mean to "strive about words to no profit" (verse 14)?

_____
_____
_____
_____
_____
_____

[Charge] them before the Lord not to strive about words to no profit. (2 Timothy 2:14)

2. How does striving about words get in the way of our teachability?

_____
_____
_____
_____
_____
_____

3. How would you tell the difference between a fruitful debate about God's Word and striving about words to no profit?

_____
_____
_____
_____
_____

4. What does it mean to rightly divide the word of truth (see verse 15)? How does that relate to teachability?

_____
_____
_____
_____
_____
_____

5. What is one way you can improve how you interact with others about biblical teaching or other ideas?

_____
_____
_____
_____
_____
_____

Day 4

1. Read Proverbs 2:1–5. Look especially at the verbs in verses 1–2: *receive, treasure, incline, apply.* What attitudes about wisdom do these verbs convey?

_____
_____
_____
_____
_____

2. Why is it important to "cry out" for discernment (verse 3)?

_____
_____
_____
_____
_____

3. What do you think it looks like in practice to seek wisdom as if it were hidden treasure?

_____
_____
_____
_____
_____

4. What does "the fear of the LORD" (verse 5) mean to you? Why is that an essential trait to possess to be teachable?

_____
_____
_____
_____
_____
_____

Then you will understand the fear of the LORD, and find the knowledge of God. (Proverbs 2:5)

5. How can you put into practice the attitudes that are encouraged by this passage?

_____
_____
_____
_____
_____

Day 5

1. Read Proverbs 2:6–9. What valuable things does the Lord offer?

_____
_____
_____
_____
_____

For the LORD gives wisdom; from His mouth come knowledge and understanding; He stores up sound wisdom for the upright; He is a shield to those who walk uprightly; He guards the paths of justice, and preserves the way of His saints. Then you will understand righteousness and justice, equity and every good path. (Proverbs 2:6–9)

2. Why do those things come only to the person who is teachable?

_____
_____
_____

3. What is the value of understanding righteousness and justice?

_____
_____
_____
_____
_____

4. What is the most important thing you have learned about teachability this week?

_____
_____
_____
_____
_____

5. How are you putting that into practice?

_____

_____

_____

_____

_____

Prayer for the Week

Dear Lord, help me to be teachable. I want to respond to Your gentle guidance and not require drastic events to happen in order to learn. I want to approach Your guidance with humility and a passionate thirst to know how to live well. Help me to withstand the temptation to be proud and measure everything by the standard of my own preferences and interests. Help me to look to You first and last for the standard of what is right. In our Lord Jesus' name. Amen. ✳

A Lesson About
Receiving the Word

To you it has been given to know the mysteries of the kingdom of God,
but to the rest it is given in parables.

LUKE 8:10

Main Objectives

In this study, you will (1) look at how we can cultivate hearts that are prepared to follow Christ, and (2) examine ways to seek God's intervention to make our shallow, weedy, and rebellious hearts open to His Word.

Read and Review

Read chapter 2 from *Parables* and answer the questions that follow. If you're meeting in a small group, you might want to have someone read each of the following excerpts from *Parables* aloud before you discuss the questions related to it.

A Surprisingly Simple Story

*The point of the parable [told in Luke 8:4–15] has to do with the soil. You cannot get the gist of this parable without understanding that the soil is a picture of the human heart. Specifically, the parable highlights four different kinds of hearts in varying degrees of receptivity. Luke 8:12 gives incontrovertible proof that the soil in the parable represents the human heart: "Those by the wayside are the ones who hear; then the devil comes and takes away the word **out of their hearts**, lest they should believe and be saved" (emphasis added).*

The seed represents the **Word of God**, and . . . the plowed field represents a human **heart** properly prepared to **receive** the Word. (*Parables*, page 26)

15

Heart: The emotional or
moral as distinguished
from the intellectual nature.
(Merriam-Webster)

*That word **hearts** makes a proper interpretation of the parable fairly easy.
The heart is, of course, where the seed of God's Word ought to take root. In the words
of Luke 8:15: "the good **ground** are those who, having heard the word with a noble
and **good heart**, keep it and bear fruit with patience" (emphasis added).*

*So the parable is about hearts in assorted stages of preparedness. All four kinds
of soil consist of the same minerals. They are organically and intrinsically identical.
What makes them distinct from one another is whether they are in a suitable condition for producing fruit or not. (Parables, page 27)*

1. What does the *heart* represent in this biblical context? Is it purely the
seat of human emotions? Explain.

_____

_____

_____

_____

*I will give them one heart, and I
will put a new spirit within them,
and take the stony heart out of
their flesh, and give them a heart
of flesh. (Ezekiel 11:19)*

2. Why does God care about the state of our hearts? Why not just focus
on our behavior?

_____

_____

_____

_____

3. Why is it important to understand that the four types of soil (hearts)
are "organically and intrinsically identical"?

_____

_____

_____

_____

Put to the Test

*The ones on the rock are
those who, when they hear, receive
the word with joy; and these have
no root, who believe for a while and
in time of temptation fall away.
(Luke 8:13)*

*The Greek word translated **temptation** in Luke 8:13 can also refer to a trial or
a test—and that is clearly the sense here. The new disciple's faith will eventually
be put to the test under the threat of persecution, by one of life's calamities, or
by the sheer difficulty of maintaining the pretense of deep, abiding belief. If it's
superficial, rootless, heartless faith, no matter how enthusiastic the response may
have seemed in the beginning, that person will "fall away"—meaning she will
abandon the faith completely. . . .*

*Those whose faith is merely temporary hear the gospel and respond, quickly
and superficially. Perhaps they have some selfish motive (thinking Jesus will fix
their worldly problems or make life easy for them). They don't truly count the cost.
For a while they bask in some emotion—a feeling of relief, exhilaration, euphoria,*

or whatever. There are tears of joy, embraces, high fives, and a lot of activity—at first. That tends to convince other believers that this is a true conversion, well rooted in genuine conviction. We might even be inclined to think that's a better response than the quiet restraint of some genuine believer who is so deeply convicted about his sin and unworthiness that all he feels is a profound sense of meekness and quiet gratitude. (Parables, pages 31–32)

Temptation: Something that causes a strong urge or desire to have or do something. (*Merriam-Webster*)

4. How does suffering put our faith to the test? What responses to suffering display faith? What responses show a person who isn't really rooted in genuine faith?

_____

_____

_____

_____

_____

We also glory in tribulations, knowing that tribulation produces perseverance; and perseverance, character; and character, hope. (Romans 5:3–4)

5. Why would anyone maintain the pretense of belief in God when he or she does not really believe? What might someone get out of that stance, at least for a while?

_____

_____

_____

_____

_____

_____

6. Why is an emotional response to the gospel not a good gauge of how real a person's commitment to Christ is?

_____

_____

_____

_____

_____

As **Jesus** makes clear in our parable, great **joy** sometimes accompanies **false** conversion. (*Parables*, page 32)

The Weeds and Thorns

The third type of soil, the weedy soil, represents a heart too enthralled or too preoccupied with worldly matters. . . . This person is too in love with this world—too obsessed with the "cares, riches, and pleasures of life"—this life (Luke 8:14). That's the key. The values of the temporal world (sinful pleasures, earthly ambitions, money, prestige, and a host of trivial diversions) deluge the heart and muffle the truth of God's Word. . . . That is precisely what the weeds and thorns in the parable represent: selfishness, sinful desire, and the unholy belief system that dominates this world. (Parables, page 33–34)

Now the ones that fell among thorns are those who, when they have heard, go out and are choked with cares, riches, and pleasures of life, and bring no fruit to maturity. (Luke 8:14)

We do not look at the things which are seen, but at the things which are not seen.
(2 Corinthians 4:18)

7. What is wrong with being too preoccupied with the cares, riches, and pleasures of life?

_____

_____

_____

_____

_____

8. As a practical matter, how do we know when our appropriate care for our earthly responsibilities crosses the line into preoccupation with worldly concerns?

_____

_____

_____

_____

_____

We know that we are of God, and the whole world lies under the sway of the wicked one. (1 John 5:19)

9. What are some of the tenets of the unholy belief system that dominates the world?

_____

_____

_____

_____

_____

Make the Connection

Read the following Scripture passages and answer the questions provided. If you are meeting in a small group, you might want to have someone read each passage aloud before you discuss the questions related to it.

The fact that Christ taught **mysteries** in parables was not to suggest that His message was meant for **elite** disciples or that it should be kept **secret**. . . . Still, only those with **eyes to see** will see it. (*MacArthur Bible Commentary*, page 1292)

When a great multitude had gathered, and they had come to Him from every city, He spoke by a parable: "A sower went out to sow his seed. And as he sowed, some fell by the wayside; and it was trampled down, and the birds of the air devoured it. Some fell on rock; and as soon as it sprang up, it withered away because it lacked moisture. And some fell among thorns, and the thorns sprang up with it and choked it. But others fell on good ground, sprang up, and yielded a crop a hundredfold." When He had said these things He cried, "He who has ears to hear, let him hear!"

Then His disciples asked Him, saying, "What does this parable mean?"

And He said . . . "Now the parable is this: The seed is the word of God. Those by the wayside are the ones who hear; then the devil comes and takes away the word out of their hearts, lest they should believe and be saved. But the ones on the rock are those who, when they hear, receive the word with joy; and these have no root, who believe for a while and in time of temptation fall away. Now the ones that fell among thorns are those who, when they have heard, go out and are choked with cares, riches, and pleasures of life, and bring no fruit to maturity. But the ones that fell on the good ground are those who, having heard the word with a noble and good heart, keep it and bear fruit with patience." (Luke 8:4–15)

10. How would you summarize the main point Jesus is trying to make in this parable?

_____

_____

_____

_____

_____

11. Have you ever experienced a pull toward being one of the kinds of unfruitful soil? If so, which kind? How did that manifest itself in your life?

_____

_____

_____

_____

_____

_____

12. To be fruitful soil, we need "a noble and good heart." This is ultimately a gift from God, but what is our part of the process of acquiring and cultivating it? What, if anything, can we do to have a good and noble heart?

_____

_____

_____

_____

_____

_____

[Jesus said,] "He who has ears to hear, let him hear!"

And the disciples came and said to Him, "Why do You speak to them in parables?"

He answered and said to them, "Because it has been given to you to know the mysteries of the kingdom of heaven, but to them it has not been given. For whoever has, to him more will be given, and he will have abundance; but whoever does not have, even what he has will be taken away from him. Therefore I speak to them in parables, because seeing they do not see, and hearing they do not hear, nor do they understand. And in them the prophecy of Isaiah is fulfilled, which says:

"**Heard**" is a reference to understanding and believing. "**Keep**" refers to ongoing obedience. "**Fruit**" is good works. . . . This constitutes **evidence** of true **salvation**. (*MacArthur Bible Commentary*, page 1292)

Perseverance *with* **fruit** *is the necessary sign of genuine, saving* **trust** *in Christ.* (*Parables*, page 36)

Jesus clearly affirms that the ability to **comprehend** spiritual truth is a gracious **gift** of God, bestowed sovereignly on the **elect**. (*MacArthur Bible Commentary*, page 1148)

Isaiah's message was to be God's **instrument** for hiding the **truth** from an unreceptive people. Centuries later, Jesus' **parables** were to do the same. (*MacArthur Bible Commentary*, page 766)

'Hearing you will hear and shall not understand,
And seeing you will see and not perceive;
For the hearts of this people have grown dull.
Their ears are hard of hearing,
And their eyes they have closed,
Lest they should see with their eyes and hear with their ears,
Lest they should understand with their hearts and turn,
So that I should heal them.'

But blessed are your eyes for they see, and your ears for they hear; for assuredly, I say to you that many prophets and righteous men desired to see what you see, and did not see it, and to hear what you hear, and did not hear it." (Matthew 13:9–17)

13. How do we demonstrate that we have ears to hear Jesus' teaching?

_____

_____

_____

_____

By revelation He made known to me the mystery . . . which in other ages was not made known to the sons of men. (Ephesians 3:3, 5)

14. What are the "mysteries of the kingdom of heaven" (verse 11)?

_____

_____

_____

_____

For everyone to whom much is given, from him much will be required; and to whom much has been committed, of him they will ask the more. (Luke 12:48)

15. What did Jesus mean when He said, "For whoever has, to him more will be given, and he will have abundance; but whoever does not have, even what he has will be taken away from him" (verse 12)?

_____

_____

_____

_____

_____

Explore the Key Points

Take some time to consider how some of the big ideas of this chapter intersect with your own life. It will be helpful to answer these questions on your own before you discuss them with your group. If you're meeting with a group, you may want to have someone read aloud the key point before you discuss it.

The Fruit We're Meant to Bear

In the parable, Jesus says that good soil will bear fruit. This fruit includes the fruit of the Spirit—"love, joy, peace, longsuffering, kindness, goodness, faithfulness, gentleness, self-control" (Galatians 5:22–23). It encompasses all "the fruits of righteousness which are by Jesus Christ, to the glory and praise of God" (Philippians 1:11). "The fruits of righteousness" means the moral conduct of those who have been declared righteous—ethical living is one kind of fruit that good soil produces. Also, good soil will produce worship: "The fruit of . . . lips, giving thanks to His name" (Hebrews 13:15). And the apostle Paul spoke of people whom he had led to Christ as fruit of his ministry (see Romans 1:13).

All of these are examples of the kinds of fruit Jesus had in mind when He said the good soil represents people who "bear fruit with patience." This fruit will be abundant and obvious in our lives—we shouldn't have to search for a few meager bits of it. The fruit we bear should be copious and sprout up from a well-cultivated heart.

16. What kinds of fruit are abundant in your life? What kinds are less abundant? (If you don't know, ask someone who knows you well!)

_____

_____

_____

_____

_____

17. We don't bear fruit by trying harder but by yielding to the working of God in the soil of our hearts. In your experience, what is your main barrier to fruitfulness? Busyness? The pursuit of wealth? The pursuit of pleasure? Explain.

_____

_____

_____

_____

_____

18. When you examine your life, do you tend to be too self-critical, too self-indulgent, or are you generally even-handed? Are you too hard on yourself or not hard enough?

_____

_____

_____

_____

Fruit of the Spirit: Godly attitudes that characterize the lives of only those who belong to God by faith in Christ and possess the Spirit of God. (*MacArthur Bible Commentary*, page 1676)

It is God who works in you both to will and to do for His good pleasure. (Philippians 2:13)

Examine me, O LORD, and prove me; try my mind and my heart. (Psalm 26:2)

The Power to Bear Fruit

It is our duty to have a prepared heart, ready to "receive with meekness the implanted word" (James 1:21)—and then nurture that seed to full fruitfulness. The Old Testament tells us that Rehoboam, Solomon's foolish son and heir to the throne, "did evil, because he did not *prepare* his heart to seek the LORD" (2 Chronicles 12:14, emphasis added). In addition, to the backslidden people of Judah in Old Testament Israel, God gave this command: "Break up your fallow ground, and do not sow among thorns" (Jeremiah 4:3). The context makes it clear that God was commanding them to prepare their hearts to receive the word (see verse 4).

But we cannot accomplish that for ourselves. We are already hopelessly unclean. We are fallen, guilty sinners with shallow, weedy, rebellious hearts. Left to ourselves, we would just grow harder. Every exposure to the light would bake in the hardness even more, until we were as impervious to God's Word as a concrete walkway is to grass seed.

Only God Himself can plow and prepare a heart to receive the Word. He does this through the regenerating and sanctifying work of His Holy Spirit, who convicts the world "of sin, and of righteousness, and of judgment" (John 16:8). He indwells His people and motivates them unto righteousness (see Ezekiel 36:27). He engraves the truth of God on their hearts (see Jeremiah 31:33; 2 Corinthians 3:3). He pours the love of God into their hearts (see Romans 5:5).

We who believe in Christ are totally dependent on the indwelling Spirit's work in our hearts to keep us tender, receptive, and ultimately fruitful. And we must remain faithfully dependent on Him.

19. How do you go about remaining faithfully dependent on the Holy Spirit to keep your heart tender, receptive, and ultimately fruitful?

_____

_____

_____

_____

_____

_____

20. Why is it important to remind ourselves that we are fallen, guilty sinners with shallow, weedy, rebellious hearts?

_____

_____

_____

_____

_____

_____

21. Describe a time in your life when God was at work in your heart, preparing it to be receptive and ultimately fruitful. What was going on in your life then?

He who began a good work in you will perfect it. (Philippians 1:6)

_____

_____

_____

_____

_____

Living the Parable

We've covered a lot in this lesson. Now it is your chance to pull it all together and decide what is the most important principle(s) you need to take to heart. You probably can't change your life in half a dozen ways this week, so prayerfully consider what is God's top priority for you.

22. What is your main takeaway(s) from this lesson? What do you want to take to heart as you go forward?

_____

_____

_____

_____

_____

23. What are some things you will do to apply what you've learned?

_____

_____

_____

_____

_____

Reflect and Respond

At the end of each lesson, you will find suggested Scripture readings for spending time alone with God during five days of the coming week. Each day of this week's readings will deal with the theme of our heart. Read the passage slowly, pausing to think about what is being said. Rather than approaching this as an assignment to complete, think of it as an encounter with your heavenly Father. Use any of the questions that are helpful.

It is each person's **duty** to have a prepared heart, ready to "receive with **meekness** the implanted word" (James 1:21)—and then to **nurture** that seed to full fruitfulness. (_Parables_, pages 36–37)

Day 1

I will give you a new heart and put a new spirit within you; I will take the heart of stone out of your flesh and give you a heart of flesh.
(Ezekiel 36:26)

1. Read Ezekiel 36:26–27. What does God promise in these verses? What does it mean to have a "new heart," "a heart of flesh"?

_____

_____

_____

_____

_____

2. According to these verses, what will we do when God gives us hearts of flesh and fills us with His Holy Spirit?

_____

_____

_____

_____

_____

I will put My Spirit within you and cause you to walk in My statutes, and you will keep My judgments and do them. (Ezekiel 36:27)

3. What are some examples of the statutes God refers to in verse 27? (Look at Matthew 5–7 for ideas.)

_____

_____

_____

_____

_____

4. Why is it significant that we can't soften our own hearts, but instead we need God to give us hearts of flesh?

_____

_____

_____

_____

_____

5. What is your heart of flesh guiding you to do in response to this passage?

_____

_____

_____

_____

_____

Day 2

1. Read Hebrews 4:12–13. In what ways does the Word of God expose the thoughts and intents of a person's heart?

_____

_____

_____

_____

_____

The word of God is living and powerful, and sharper than any two-edged sword, piercing even to the division of soul and spirit, and of joints and marrow, and is a discerner of the thoughts and intents of the heart. (Hebrews 4:12)

2. What is an example of a thought or intention of the heart that the Word might expose?

_____

_____

_____

_____

_____

_____

3. When has the Word of God exposed the thoughts and intents of *your* heart? How did that help you?

_____

_____

_____

_____

_____

_____

_____

4. How should we live in light of what the Word of God can do with our hearts?

_____

_____

_____

_____

_____

_____

5. Do you like the fact that nothing is hidden from God's sight, or does it sometimes bother you? Explain.

_____

_____

_____

_____

_____

There is no creature hidden from His sight, but all things are naked and open to the eyes of Him to whom we must give account. (Hebrews 4:13)

Day 3

*Do not fear, little flock, for it is
your Father's good pleasure to
give you the kingdom. Sell what
you have and give alms; provide
yourselves money bags which do not
grow old, a treasure in the heavens
that does not fail, where no thief
approaches nor moth destroys.*
(Luke 12:32–33)

1. Read Luke 12:32–34. What does this passage instruct us to do?

_____

_____

_____

_____

_____

2. What reason for doing this does it give? How would you put this into your own words?

_____

_____

_____

_____

_____

_____

*For where your treasure is,
there your heart will be also.*
(Luke 12:34)

3. When have you experienced your heart being where your treasure is?

_____

_____

_____

_____

_____

4. Is it possible to have wealth and yet not have your heart overly attached to your money? If so, how? If not, why not?

_____

_____

_____

_____

_____

_____

5. What are you moved to do in response to this passage?

_____

_____

_____

_____

_____

_____

Day 4

1. Read James 4:7–8. In what sense is purifying our hearts something that is our responsibility to do?

_____
_____
_____
_____
_____
_____

Submit to God. Resist the devil and he will flee from you. Draw near to God and He will draw near to you. Cleanse your hands, you sinners; and purify your hearts, you double-minded. (James 4:7–8)

2. How do we purify our hearts?

_____
_____
_____
_____
_____
_____

3. Read Psalm 51:10. In what sense is creating a clean heart something only God can do?

_____
_____
_____
_____
_____
_____
_____
_____

Create in me a clean heart, O God, and renew a steadfast spirit within me. (Psalm 51:10)

4. In what ways can you cooperate with God today in the cleansing of your heart?

_____
_____
_____
_____
_____
_____

5. Read Proverbs 4:23. Why is it important to keep our hearts with diligence?

_____
_____
_____
_____
_____

Watch over your heart with all diligence, for from it flow the springs of life (Proverbs 4:23 NASB)

Day 5

Whatever enters the mouth goes into the stomach and is eliminated. . . . But those things which proceed out of the mouth come from the heart, and they defile a man (Matthew 15:16–17)

1. Read Matthew 15:16–20. Why can't we be defiled by what goes into our mouths, even if we eat with unwashed hands?

_____

_____

_____

_____

2. When has something defiling come out of your heart? How did it manifest itself?

_____

_____

_____

_____

3. What good things can come out of our hearts?

_____

_____

_____

_____

For out of the heart proceed evil thoughts, murders, adulteries, fornications, thefts, false witness, blasphemies. (Matthew 15:19)

4. What should we do when we find something bad comes out of our hearts? What should we not do?

_____

_____

_____

_____

5. What are the most important things you have learned from this week's study of the heart?

_____

_____

_____

_____

Prayer for the Week

Dear Lord, thank You for giving me a heart of flesh. Please fill me with Your Spirit so I will keep Your commands. Reveal the thoughts and intentions of my heart so they can be conformed to Your own intentions. Create in me a clean heart, and show me how to cooperate with that process. If my treasure is luring my heart away from putting Your agenda first, please let me know that. And if anything in my heart is defiling me, please show me so that I can be honest about it and not hide it. I want my heart to give glory to You. In our Lord Jesus' name. Amen. ✳

A Lesson About the Cost of Discipleship

For which of you, intending to build a tower, does not sit down first and count the cost, whether he has enough to finish it.

LUKE 14:28

Main Objectives

In this study, you will (1) look at what Jesus said about the true value of the kingdom of God, and (2) seek to understand and embrace the cost of following Christ.

Read and Review

Read chapter 3 from *Parables* and answer the questions that follow. If you're meeting in a small group, you might want to have someone read each of the following excerpts from *Parables* aloud before you discuss the questions related to it.

Defining the Kingdom of God

The kingdom of heaven is a frequent theme in Jesus' parables. It is the realm over which Christ Himself is the undisputed King of kings and Lord of lords. It is the domain in which His lordship is even now fully operative. In other words, all who truly belong to the kingdom of heaven have formally yielded to Christ's lordship. . . .

[Jesus' bodily return to usher in the kingdom in its fullness] is what Jesus taught us to pray for: "Your kingdom come. Your will be done on earth as it is in heaven"

At present, the kingdom is a **spiritual** dominion. . . . The earthly culmination of the kingdom awaits His bodily **return.** (*Parables*, page 40)

Kingdom: A country whose ruler is a king or queen; the spiritual world of which God is king. (*Merriam-Webster*)

(Matthew 6:10). *When the kingdom is finally manifest in the new creation, it will be visible, universal (spanning heaven and earth), and never ending. In the meantime, the kingdom is absolutely real; it is present; and it is constantly, quietly growing, as sinners are redeemed and graciously granted kingdom citizenship for all eternity.* (*Parables*, pages 40–41)

1. How would you define the kingdom of God (or kingdom of heaven) in your own words?

_____

_____

_____

_____

_____

Jesus came to Galilee, preaching the gospel of the kingdom of God, and saying, "The time is fulfilled, and the kingdom of God is at hand. Repent, and believe. (Mark 1:14–15)

2. Why is it a privilege to belong to God's kingdom?

_____

_____

_____

_____

3. What are the responsibilities of being a citizen of God's kingdom?

_____

_____

_____

_____

_____

The Cost of the Kingdom

Lamb of God: A lamb was offered in the daily **sacrifices** of Israel. . . . John the Baptist used this expression as a reference to the **ultimate** sacrifice of Jesus on the cross to **atone** for the **sins** of the world. (*MacArthur Bible Commentary*, page 1349)

We could sooner buy all the palaces and mansions on earth than we could earn entry into the kingdom of heaven by our own merits. In fact, the characteristic attitude of all true kingdom citizens is that they are "poor in spirit" (Matthew 5:3). They recognize and confess their own utter spiritual poverty. They know that they are unworthy sinners (1 Timothy 1:15). . . .

That's why Jesus—the perfect, spotless, sinless Lamb of God—had to make the only possible atonement for sinners. "[God] made Him who knew no sin to be sin for us, that we might become the righteousness of God in Him" (2 Corinthians 5:21). In effect, Christ paid the kingdom's entry fee in full for those who believe on His name—because He is the only one who could ever pay such an unimaginably high price.

And it was indeed an exorbitant price—worth infinitely more than all earth's gold and material riches combined. "You were not redeemed with corruptible things, like silver or gold . . . but with the precious blood of Christ, as of a lamb without blemish and without spot" (1 Peter 1:18–19). . . . Therefore all who enter the kingdom do so freely, "without money and without price" (Isaiah 55:1), by grace through faith—not by any merit or virtue of their own (Ephesians 2:8–9). (Parables, pages 42–43)

4. What does it mean to be "poor in spirit"?

_____

_____

_____

_____

Blessed are the poor in spirit, for theirs is the kingdom of heaven. (Matthew 5:3)

5. How did Christ pay our entry fee to the kingdom of heaven?

_____

_____

_____

_____

6. Why do we say that Christ's blood is "precious"?

_____

_____

_____

_____

The life of the flesh is in the blood . . . it is the blood that makes atonement for the soul. (Leviticus 17:11)

Considering the Cost

Genuine faith never fails to appreciate the true cost of salvation—what our deliverance from sin's curse and bondage cost Christ; what it means to be bought by Christ and bow to His lordship; and (above all) how valuable redemption is in terms of its eternal worth to the sinner.

*Further, and paradoxically, though the Lord Jesus paid the price in full, it is **not** inconsistent to urge people to count the cost of entering the kingdom. That is, in fact, the very point Jesus is making in these two brief parables recorded in Matthew 13:44–46. He urges all who would enter the kingdom to consider what it will cost them. (Parables, page 43)*

Salvation: The act of saving someone from sin or evil; the state of being saved from sin or evil; something that saves someone or something from danger or a difficult situation. (*Merriam-Webster*)

7. What did our deliverance from sin's curse and bondage cost Christ?

_____

_____

_____

_____

For He made Him who knew no sin to be sin for us, that we might become the righteousness of God in Him. (2 Corinthians 5:21)

8. What eternal worth do we get when we enter the kingdom of heaven?

_____

_____

_____

_____

9. What price are you willing to pay for the eternal worth of the kingdom? Is there any price you're not willing to pay? Explain.

_____

_____

_____

_____

_____

Make the Connection

Read the following Scripture passages and answer the questions provided. If you are meeting in a small group, you might want to have someone read each passage aloud before you discuss the questions related to it.

[Jesus said,] "Again, the kingdom of heaven is like treasure hidden in a field, which a man found and hid; and for joy over it he goes and sells all that he has and buys that field. Again, the kingdom of heaven is like a merchant seeking beautiful pearls, who, when he had found one pearl of great price, went and sold all that he had and bought it." (Matthew 13:44–46)

10. What main point does Jesus make with His parable of the hidden treasure?

_____

_____

_____

_____

_____

11. What point does Jesus make with His parable of the pearl? How is it similar to the point of the earlier parable? How is it different?

_____

_____

_____

_____

_____

12. How does it affect the way a person lives if he of she treats the kingdom of heaven like something of surpassing value?

_____

_____

_____

_____

These two parables have **identical** meanings. Both picture salvation as something **hidden** from most people but so **valuable** that people who have it revealed to them are willing to give up **all they have** to possess it. (*MacArthur Bible Commentary*, page 1150)

In Jesus' time, pearls were the equivalent of **diamonds** today. Well-formed pearls were as valuable as any **precious gem**. Pearls also made wealth very portable. If you had fine pearls, you owned a **fortune**. (*Parables*, page 47)

Now great multitudes went with Him. And He turned and said to them "If anyone comes to Me and does not hate his father and mother, wife and children, brothers and sisters, yes, and his own life also, he cannot be My disciple. And whoever does not bear his cross and come after Me cannot be My disciple. For which of you, intending to build a tower, does not sit down first and count the cost, whether he has enough to finish it—lest, after he has laid the foundation, and is not able to finish, all who see it begin to mock him, saying, 'This man began to build and was not able to finish'? Or what king, going to make war against another king, does not sit down first and consider whether he is able with ten thousand to meet him who comes against him with twenty thousand? Or else, while the other is still a great way off, he sends a delegation and asks conditions of peace. So likewise, whoever of you does not forsake all that he has cannot be My disciple." (Luke 14:25–33)

The "hatred" called for here is actually a **lesser love**. Jesus was calling His disciples to cultivate such a **devotion** to Him that their attachment to everything else—including their own lives—would seem like hatred **by comparison**. (*MacArthur Bible Commentary*, page 1308)

13. What point does Jesus make by using the examples of the person building the tower and the king facing war?

_____

_____

_____

_____

_____

14. What are some potential costs of following Jesus that Christ talks about in this passage?

_____

_____

_____

_____

15. How do you respond to those potential costs? Are you willing to pay that much for the privilege of following Christ? Why or why not?

_____

_____

_____

_____

Genuine **faith** is not a mere idea or a selective acquiescence to Jesus' teaching. It means letting go of **everything** else and giving up all trust that anything or anyone else can gain us **merit** with God. (*Parables*, page 53)

Explore the Key Points

Take some time to consider how some of the big ideas of this chapter intersect with your own life. It will be helpful to answer these questions on your own before you discuss them with your group. If you're meeting with a group, you may want to have someone read aloud the key point before you discuss it.

The Kingdom's Priceless Value

In Christ and His kingdom we have an eternal treasure that is rich beyond comparison. This treasure is incorruptible, undefiled, unfading, eternal, and reserved in heaven for believers (see 1 Peter 1:4). The kingdom is a realm of blessedness and harmony where no one quarrels to get his or her own way and where people gladly do what Christ would do if He were in their shoes.

The kingdom consists of everything that is eternal, everything that has true and intrinsic value, and everything that is permanently incorruptible and undefiled. Everything else will pass away, while the blessedness of the kingdom will never fade or diminish. Indeed, as Isaiah wrote, "Of the increase of [Christ's] government and peace there will be no end" (Isaiah 9:7).

The kingdom is a heavenly treasure lying in the field of this poverty-stricken, bankrupt, accursed world. It is a prize sufficient to make every one of earth's poor, miserable, blind, sinful inhabitants immeasurably rich for all eternity. The treasure includes salvation, forgiveness, love, joy, peace, virtue, goodness, glory, eternal life in heaven, the presence of God, and Christ Himself. Literally, everything of eternal value is encompassed in the treasure of the kingdom.

That is why the kingdom is the most valuable commodity that can ever be found. Only an absolute fool would be unwilling to relinquish everything he owns to gain it.

16. Has it cost you anything to be a follower of Jesus? If so, what has that cost been?

17. The man who found the treasure hidden in the field joyfully sold everything he had in order to buy that field. Do you have joy when you think about the things of eternal value you have gained from following Christ? How does thinking about salvation, forgiveness, peace, and the other treasures of the kingdom make you feel?

18. What additional price, if any, might God be asking you to pay as you follow your Lord?

_____

_____

_____

_____

_____

_____

Greater love has no one than this, than to lay down one's life for his friends. (John 15:13)

The Kingdom's Hiddenness

In the parables Jesus told in Matthew 13:44–46, the treasure was hidden in the field, and the merchant had to seek out the pearl of great price. These treasures weren't obvious to the casual observer. Likewise, the kingdom is there for those who seek it, but it does have to be sought. Someone whose interest in it is merely tepid will not take notice.

Jesus said the kingdom of God does not come with fanfare, and most pay no attention to it (see Luke 17:20). Paul wrote, "The natural man does not receive the things of the Spirit of God, for they are foolishness to him; nor can he know them, because they are spiritually discerned" (1 Corinthians 2:14). Jesus also said that "unless one is born again, he cannot see the kingdom of God" (John 3:3). The kingdom and its worth remain hidden from carnal minds, which is why many do not esteem the treasure of salvation or even discover it.

This also explains why worldly people don't understand or appreciate why Christians are passionate about the glory of God. They don't understand why we prize the kingdom of heaven so highly when it means nothing to them. Unregenerate people simply have no sense of what divine glory entails. They can't fathom why someone would willingly submit to the lordship of Jesus Christ. They don't understand why anyone would repudiate sin and its pleasures in order to pursue righteousness, or sacrifice earthly delights for heavenly joys. These things go against every instinct and every desire of the fallen human heart.

Now when [Jesus] was asked by the Pharisees when the kingdom of God would come, He answered them and said, "The kingdom of God does not come with observation." (Luke 17:20)

19. Have you experienced unbelievers who can't appreciate why you're passionate about God's glory? If so, how has that affected you?

_____

_____

_____

_____

_____

Through **illumination** of the Word, the Holy Spirit provides His saints the capacity to discern **divine truth**, which the spiritually dead are **unable** to comprehend. (*MacArthur Bible Commentary*, page 1568)

Jesus answered, "Most assuredly, I say to you, unless one is born of water and the Spirit, he cannot enter the kingdom of God.
(John 3:5)

20. How did you come to enter the kingdom of heaven? Were you seeking God, or did He just orchestrate circumstances so you learned of the gospel and responded? Explain.

_____

_____

_____

_____

_____

The god of this world has blinded the minds of the unbelieving so that they might not see the light of the gospel.
(2 Corinthians 4:4 NASB)

21. Who in your world needs your prayers for God to unblind their eyes and prepare their soil to receive the truth about Him? How can you be instrumental in their lives to pique their curiosity about the things of God?

_____

_____

_____

_____

_____

Living the Parable

We've covered a lot in this lesson. Now it is your chance to pull it all together and decide what is the most important principle(s) you need to take to heart. You probably can't change your life in half a dozen ways this week, so prayerfully consider what is God's top priority for you.

22. What is your main takeaway(s) from this lesson? What do you want to take to heart as you go forward?

_____

_____

_____

_____

_____

23. What are some things you will do to apply what you've learned?

_____

_____

_____

_____

Reflect and Respond

At the end of each lesson, you will find suggested Scripture readings for spending time alone with God during five days of the coming week. Each day of this week's readings will deal with the theme of the precious value of what we have received in the kingdom of God. Read each passage slowly, pausing to think about what is being said. Rather than approaching this as an assignment to complete, think of it as an encounter with your heavenly Father. Use any of the questions that are helpful.

*Count the **cost** of following [Jesus]. And if you do that thoughtfully, you will surely realize that the pearl is so **valuable** and the **treasure** so rich that it is worth letting go of every temporal treasure. (Parables, page 55)*

Day 1

1. Read Ephesians 1:3–6. What spiritual blessings does Paul list in this passage (see verse 3)?

   _____

   _____

   _____

   _____

Blessed be the God and Father of our Lord Jesus Christ, who has blessed us with every spiritual blessing in the heavenly places in Christ. (Ephesians 1:3)

2. What has God done to make us "holy and without blame before Him in love" (verse 4)? Why should we value this blessing? What would the alternative be?

   _____

   _____

   _____

   _____

   _____

He chose us in Him before the foundation of the world, that we should be holy and without blame before Him in love. (Ephesians 1:4)

3. What does our spiritual adoption as sons of God give us (see verse 5)? What rights does the heir in a family have that outsiders don't have?

   _____

   _____

   _____

   _____

   _____

Having predestined us to adoption as sons by Jesus Christ to Himself, according to the good pleasure of His will. (Ephesians 1:5)

4. What does it mean that we are "accepted in the Beloved" (verse 6)? Why is that of value to us?

   _____

   _____

   _____

   _____

To the praise of the glory of His grace, by which He made us accepted in the Beloved. (Ephesians 1:6)

5. Choose one of these blessings and think about why it is especially valuable to you. What difference does this blessing make in the way you live?

_____

_____

_____

_____

_____

Day 2

In Him we have redemption through His blood, the forgiveness of sins, according to the riches of His grace. (Ephesians 1:7)

1. Read Ephesians 1:7–12. In this passage, Paul continues the list of spiritual blessings that he began in verse 3. What does "redemption through his blood" mean (verse 7)? How are we redeemed through Christ's blood?

_____

_____

_____

_____

2. Why should we be overjoyed to have our sins forgiven?

_____

_____

_____

_____

3. What is grace (see verse 7)? Why does Paul speak of "the riches of" God's grace? Why is grace something infinitely valuable?

_____

_____

_____

_____

In the dispensation of the fullness of the times He might gather together in one all things in Christ, both which are in heaven and which are on earth—in Him. (Ephesians 1:10)

4. Paul tells us that God is gathering all things together in Christ and bringing unity where before there was disharmony (see verse 10). Why should we care about this unity and harmony under Christ's lordship?

_____

_____

_____

5. Describe the "inheritance" we have been given (verse 11). Why is it infinitely valuable?

_____

_____

_____

_____

_____

In Him also we have obtained an inheritance, being predestined according to the purpose of Him who works all things according to the counsel of His will. (Ephesians 7:12)

Day 3

1. Read Ephesians 2:1–7. What was your former state before you met Christ (see verses 1–3)? Why are you glad to escape this condition?

_____

_____

_____

_____

_____

You He made alive, who were dead in trespasses and sins, in which you once walked according to the course of this world . . . we all once conducted ourselves in the lusts of our flesh, fulfilling the desires of the flesh and of the mind, and were by nature children of wrath. (Ephesians 2:1–3)

2. What does it mean to say we were "dead in sin" (verse 1)?

_____

_____

_____

_____

_____

3. What is your personal experience of being made alive in Christ? Are you aware of the difference from being dead in sin, or do you just take it on faith?

_____

_____

_____

_____

_____

4. How have you experienced God being "rich in mercy" toward you (verse 4)?

_____

_____

_____

_____

God, who is rich in mercy, because of His great love with which He loved us . . . made us alive. (Ephesians 2:4–5)

[God] raised us up together, and made us sit together in the heavenly places in Christ Jesus, that in the ages to come He might show the exceeding riches of His grace in His kindness toward us in Christ. (Ephesians 2:6–7)

5. In what sense do we as believers sit with Christ in the heavenly places (see verse 6)? In what sense were we raised when Christ was raised?

_____

_____

_____

_____

_____

_____

Day 4

You, who once were alienated and enemies in your mind by wicked works, yet now He has reconciled in the body of His flesh through death, to present you holy, and blameless, and above reproach in His sight. (Colossians 1:21–22)

1. Read Colossians 1:21–23. Why were you previously alienated from God?

_____

_____

_____

_____

_____

2. How were you reconciled to God?

_____

_____

_____

_____

_____

_____

3. Why is it infinitely valuable to be holy, blameless, and above reproach in God's sight?

_____

_____

_____

_____

_____

_____

If indeed you continue in the faith, grounded and steadfast, and are not moved away from the hope of the gospel which you heard. (Colossians 1:23)

4. In verse 23, Paul adds an "if" clause that puts a condition on what he has been saying. What is the condition? Why is it important?

_____

_____

_____

_____

_____

5. Paul speaks of "the hope of the gospel" (verse 23). How does the gospel give you hope?

_____

_____

_____

_____

_____

_____

Gospel: The message concerning Christ, the kingdom of God, and salvation. (*Merriam-Webster*)

Day 5

1. Read 2 Peter 1:3–4. According to these verses, what has God given you (see verse 3)? How would you describe what He has given in your own words?

_____

_____

_____

_____

_____

[God's] divine power has given to us all things that pertain to life and godliness, through the knowledge of Him who called us by glory and virtue. (2 Peter 1:3)

2. What are the things necessary for godliness that God has given us?

_____

_____

_____

_____

_____

_____

3. The reason we have everything necessary for godliness is because we have knowledge of God. What does it mean to *know* God? In what ways is it the same or different from knowing information *about* God?

_____

_____

_____

_____

_____

By which have been given to us exceedingly great and precious promises, that through these you may be partakers of the divine nature, having escaped the corruption that is in the world through lust. (2 Peter 1:4)

4. Peter writes that God has enabled believers to be "partakers of the divine nature" (verse 4). What does this mean?

_____

_____

_____

_____

_____

5. Why is it infinitely valuable to be a partaker of the divine nature?

_____

_____

_____

_____

_____

_____

_____

Prayer for the Week

Dear Lord, thank You for redeeming me from death, forgiving my sins, adopting me in Your family, and making me someone who causes others to praise Your glory. Thank You for reconciling me to You so I don't have the status of an enemy, even though I deserve it. Thank You for giving me everything I need to lead a godly life. Thank You that I can know You, participate in Your divine nature, and grow more like You as I get to know You better. Please help me to always be grateful for these unimaginable blessings and never take them for granted. Help me to also appreciate the value of following You, even while I count the cost of following You. In our Lord Jesus' name. Amen. ✳

A Lesson About
Justice and Grace

So the last will be first, and the first last.

MATTHEW 20:16

Main Objectives

In this study, you will (1) examine and celebrate the principle of extravagant generosity by which God treats all saved sinners, and (2) seek to become aware of feelings of jealousy when God is more generous with someone than you think that person deserves.

Read and Review

Read chapter 4 from *Parables* and answer the questions that follow. If you're meeting in a small group, you might want to have someone read each of the following excerpts from *Parables* aloud before you discuss the questions related to it.

The Principle of Grace

What we have to bear in mind is that all people are totally unworthy. No one ***deserves*** *God's favor. We are all guilty sinners who deserve nothing more than damnation. No one who has sinned has any rightful claim on the kindness of God.*

God, on the other hand, has every right to show mercy and compassion to whomever He chooses (Exodus 33:19). Furthermore, when He shows mercy it is always in lavish abundance. As He told Moses, He is "the LORD, the LORD God, merciful and gracious, longsuffering, and abounding in goodness and truth, keeping mercy for thousands, forgiving iniquity and transgression and sin" (34:6–7).

[God] said, "I will make all My goodness pass before you. . . . I will be gracious to whom I will be gracious, and I will have compassion on whom I will have compassion." (Exodus 33:19)

[Judas Iscariot] was a close **disciple** of Jesus Christ. . . . *But he lost his soul forever.* The [thief on the cross] was a hardened, lifelong **criminal** who was still mocking everything holy while being put to death for his **crimes**. *But he went straight to paradise forever.* (*Parables*, page 57)

People who protest that God is unfair or unjust when He shows grace to the least deserving people simply do not understand the principle of grace. Undiluted justice would mean immediate death for every sinner, because "the wages of sin is death" (Romans 6:23). The truth is, we don't really want what is "fair." We all desperately need grace and mercy.

*On the other hand, grace is not unjust, because Christ made full atonement for the sins of those who trust Him—and thereby turned justice in their favor. "If we confess our sins, He is faithful **and just** to forgive us our sins and to cleanse us from all unrighteousness" (1 John 1:9, emphasis added). Because Christ took the penalty of sin on Himself, God can justify believing sinners (even notorious sinners like the thief on the cross) without compromising His own righteousness. "He [is both] just and the justifier of the one who has faith in Jesus" (Romans 3:26). (Parables, page 59)*

1. Why are all people undeserving of God's favor and worthy of only damnation?

_____

_____

_____

_____

_____

By grace you have been saved through faith, and that not of yourselves; it is the gift of God. (Ephesians 2:8)

2. In what ways is God's grace not unjust?

_____

_____

_____

_____

_____

3. Are there any individuals or types of persons to whom you think God shouldn't show mercy? If so, what sort of person? If not, why not?

_____

_____

_____

_____

_____

A Change in Attitude

The expression "evil eye" [in Matthew 20:15] speaks of jealousy. And let's face it: jealousy is an intrinsic aspect of fallen human nature. Almost anyone at the end of that pay line would probably have felt some welling up of resentment. After all, those men had worked the full twelve-hour day—most of it under the hot sun, while the workers hired at 5:00 PM began work under a cooling breeze at twilight and worked for only an hour.

But we must not lose sight of the fact that when the 6:00 AM crew were hired, they were quite happy with the offer of a denarius a day. They began the workday

The word translated **"complained"** in the Greek text is *egogguzon*. It's onomatopoeic: the word itself forms a sound that evokes its meaning. It sounds like a **grumble** or muttered complaint. (*Parables*, page 65)

in high spirits, thrilled that the landowner was being supremely generous with them. He was offering more in wages than they could reasonably expect.

What changed their mood so drastically? Just that someone less deserving (or so they thought) was treated with even more generosity. Instantly they felt mistreated—envious of the other person's good fortune. Their whole attitude changed. They couldn't stand the thought that other workers would get the same pay without working as hard as they did. Suddenly their gratitude and admiration for the landowner's extreme generosity gave way to bitter resentment. (Parables, pages 65-66)

Jealousy: An unhappy or angry feeling of wanting to have what someone else has. (*Merriam-Webster*)

4. Why do we tend to be so concerned about fairness that we become jealous when God is generous to someone else?

_____

_____

_____

_____

5. What would happen if God treated all humans as we truly deserve to be treated?

As it is written: "There is none righteous, no, not one." (Romans 3:10)

_____

_____

_____

_____

6. What is Jesus' point in Matthew 20:1–15? Is He making a point about how we should run businesses and relationships today, or is He just referring to the way God runs the business of salvation? Explain.

_____

_____

_____

_____

_____

A Dead Heat

*The proverb that goes with this parable is an **indicative**, a simple statement of fact: "The last will be first, and the first last." What does that mean, and how would it work? In a foot race, for example, the only way for the last to be first and the first to be last is for everyone to finish simultaneously. If everyone crosses the finish line at exactly the same instant, the first are last and the last are first. Everyone ends in a dead heat.*

Indicative: Of, relating to, or constituting a verb form or set of verb forms that represents the denoted act or state as an objective fact. (*Merriam-Webster*)

That, of course, is precisely the point Jesus was making in the parable. Those hired first and those hired last all got exactly the same pay. All of them, from the first to the last, got the full benefit of the landowner's generosity, in equal shares.

What spiritual lesson is woven into that story?

This is the **point**: If you are a genuine believer, you receive the **full benefits** of God's immeasurable grace, just like **everyone else** in God's kingdom. (*Parables*, page 68)

*The lesson is actually quite simple: the story is a precise picture of God's sovereign saving grace. Since sinners are all unworthy, and the riches of God's grace are inexhaustible, all believers receive an infinite and eternal share of His mercy and kindness, though no one really deserves it. "In Him we [all of us] have [complete] redemption through His blood, the forgiveness of sins, according to the riches of His grace" (Ephesians 1:7). He "raised us up **together**, and made us sit together in the heavenly places in Christ Jesus, that in the ages to come He might show the exceeding riches of His grace in His kindness toward us in Christ Jesus" (2:6–7, emphasis added). That speaks of all who are redeemed. It is the Father's good pleasure to give them the kingdom (Luke 12:32)—all of them, and in equal abundance. The dying thief who repented in his final moments entered paradise, where he is enjoying eternal life and everlasting fellowship with Christ just the same as Peter, James, and John, who literally gave their lives in service to the Savior. (Parables, page 67)*

7. What does Jesus mean in Matthew 20:16 when he says, "So the last will be first, and the first last"? What does that look like in everyday life?

_____

_____

_____

_____

_____

_____

_____

But godliness is profitable for all things, having promise of the life that now is and of that which is to come.
(1 Timothy 4:8)

8. If the eternal life we receive will be the same whether we do a lot or a little to serve God in this life, why do we have any incentive to make an effort? Explain.

_____

_____

_____

_____

_____

_____

_____

For there is no partiality with God.
(Romans 2:11)

9. What can we learn about God from His decision to bless the first and the last equally?

_____

_____

_____

_____

_____

_____

_____

Make the Connection

Read the following Scripture passages and answer the questions provided. If you are meeting in a small group, you might want to have someone read each passage aloud before you discuss the questions related to it.

[Jesus said,] "But many who are first will be last, and the last first.

"For the kingdom of heaven is like a landowner who went out early in the morning to hire laborers for his vineyard. Now when he had agreed with the laborers for a denarius a day, he sent them into his vineyard. And he went out about the third hour and saw others standing idle in the marketplace, and said to them, 'You also go into the vineyard, and whatever is right I will give you.' So they went. Again he went out about the sixth and the ninth hour, and did likewise. And about the eleventh hour he went out and found others standing idle, and said to them, 'Why have you been standing here idle all day?' They said to him, 'Because no one hired us.' He said to them, 'You also go into the vineyard, and whatever is right you will receive.'

"So when evening had come, the owner of the vineyard said to his steward, 'Call the laborers and give them their wages, beginning with the last to the first.' And when those came who were hired about the eleventh hour, they each received a denarius. But when the first came, they supposed that they would receive more; and they likewise received each a denarius. And when they had received it, they complained against the landowner, saying, 'These last men have worked only one hour, and you made them equal to us who have borne the burden and the heat of the day.' But he answered one of them and said, 'Friend, I am doing you no wrong. Did you not agree with me for a denarius? Take what is yours and go your way. I wish to give to this last man the same as to you. Is it not lawful for me to do what I wish with my own things? Or is your eye evil because I am good?' But many who are first will be last, and the last first." (Matthew 19:30–20:16)

Such hiring was typical during **harvest**. Day laborers stood in the market place from dawn, **hoping** to be hired for the day's work. (*MacArthur Bible Commentary*, page 1161)

The man is acting **graciously** to those whom he overpaid. This payment is no **slight** against those whom he paid a full wage for a full day's work. That was precisely what they **agreed to** in the beginning, but it was the landowner's privilege to extend the same **generosity** to all. (*MacArthur Bible Commentary*, page 1161)

10. On what basis are the workers in this story paid for their labor?

_____

_____

_____

_____

_____

11. Why were the workers hired in the early morning angry at receiving only a denarius?

_____

_____

_____

_____

_____

_____

Denarius: A typical day's pay for a soldier serving in the Roman army . . . a respectable living wage. (*Parables*, page 62)

He who hears My word and believes in Him who sent Me has everlasting life. (John 5:24)

12. Where would you place yourself in this story? For example, imagine that a notorious sinner whom you know personally repented at the end of his life and embraced Christ. Would you be thrilled or bothered that such a person had the same eternal reward as you? Or do you see yourself as one of those hired late in the day? Explain.

_____

_____

_____

_____

Peter points out that they have already done what Christ **demanded**. . . . They have embarked on the **life** of **faith** with Christ. Note that Jesus does not rebuke Peter for his **expectation** of reward. (*MacArthur Bible Commentary*, page 1161)

Then Peter answered and said to Him, "See, we have left all and followed You. Therefore what shall we have?"

So Jesus said to them, "Assuredly I say to you, that in the regeneration, when the Son of Man sits on the throne of His glory, you who have followed Me will also sit on twelve thrones, judging the twelve tribes of Israel. And everyone who has left houses or brothers or sisters or father or mother or wife or children or lands, for My name's sake, shall receive a hundredfold, and inherit eternal life. But many who are first will be last, and the last first." (Matthew 19:27–30)

13. What does Peter's question suggest about his view of the way things ought to work in Jesus' kingdom?

_____

_____

_____

_____

14. How does Jesus respond to Peter's assumptions in the parable of the workers in the vineyard, which follows this scene?

_____

_____

_____

_____

We all enter into the **same** eternal life. We all will receive the **same** spiritual blessings in heaven. (*Parables*, page 68)

15. Jesus said the twelve disciples would receive a great reward, and so will anyone who has left anything for His sake. Where are you in this picture? What have you left for Jesus' sake? What reward do you expect to receive?

_____

_____

_____

_____

Explore the Key Points

Take some time to consider how some of the big ideas of this chapter intersect with your own life. It will be helpful to answer these questions on your own before you discuss them with your group. If you're meeting with a group, you may want to have someone read aloud the key point before you discuss it.

God Does the Calling

In the parable of the workers in the vineyard, the landowner went to the marketplace of the world to find laborers. In the same way, it is God who does the seeking and saving of people. We don't seek and find God; He seeks and finds us. Our salvation is entirely His work, which is the main reason why we have no right to make demands or set limits on what He gives to someone else. It is God's prerogative, and His alone, to show mercy to whomever He chooses.

God has been calling people into His kingdom throughout human history and in every phase of the human lifespan. It's an ongoing work. Jesus said in John 9:4, "I must work the works of Him who sent Me while it is day; the night is coming when no one can work." Our parable illustrates what He meant. Redemption continues until the judgment comes. In fact, the reason God has waited so long for the final judgment is so He can show mercy to as many people as possible. But the day of judgment *will* come at a time of His choosing.

We love [God] because He first loved us. (1 John 4:19)

Day of Judgment: The present world system is reserved for future judgment, which will come by the Word of God. (*MacArthur Bible Commentary*, page 1940)

16. How did God call you? Did He call you through another person, through circumstances, through more than one person? Explain.

_____

_____

_____

_____

_____

_____

_____

17. If God does the calling, does that mean we don't have to worry about sharing our faith with others? Why or why not?

[Jesus] said to them, "Go into all the world and preach the gospel to every creature." (Mark 16:15)

_____

_____

_____

_____

_____

_____

_____

18. Have you ever shared your faith with someone who didn't respond positively? If so, how does it help you to know that God is the one who does the calling?

_____

_____

_____

_____

_____

_____

_____

Who God Calls

God calls people who know they are sinners, not those who think they are fine. The day laborers in the parable were desperate and knew they needed someone to offer them work. They were poor and meek, devoid of resources, begging for work—they represent the poor in spirit. There was nothing complacent or self-satisfied about them, especially those who still had nothing at the end of the day. They were the opposite of the Laodiceans in Revelation, who thought they were "'rich . . . and have need of nothing'—and do not know that [they] are wretched, miserable, poor, blind, and naked" (Revelation 3:17).

Jesus said, "Those who are well have no need of a physician, but those who are sick. I did not come to call the righteous, but sinners, to repentance" (Mark 2:17). The apostle Paul wrote, "For you see your calling, brethren, that not many wise according to the flesh, not many mighty, not many noble, are called. But God has chosen the foolish things of the world to put to shame the wise, and God has chosen the weak things of the world to put to shame the things which are mighty; and the base things of the world and the things which are despised God has chosen, and the things which are not, to bring to nothing the things that are, that no flesh should glory in His presence" (1 Corinthians 1:26–29).

God wants no one to be able to boast of deserving to be in His kingdom. So when He calls a person, His grace gives that person an awareness of being poor in spirit and desperately in need of redemption.

19. When God called you, how did He make you aware of your neediness?

_____

_____

_____

_____

_____

_____

_____

20. Are you still aware of neediness before God, or does that rarely cross your mind when you go before Him these days? Explain.

_____

_____

_____

_____

_____

He who covers his sins will not prosper. (Proverbs 28:13)

21. Think about those people in your life who do not know Christ. Which of them, do you think, have an awareness that they need help from someone outside themselves? Which of them seem self-sufficient?

_____

_____

_____

_____

_____

_____

_____

Salvation is **God's work**, not something any sinner can accomplish for **himself.** (*Parables*, page 69)

Living the Parable

You've covered a lot in this lesson. Now you will have a chance to pull it all together and decide what is the most important thing(s) you need to take to heart. You probably can't change your life in half a dozen ways this week, so what do you believe is God's top priority for you?

22. What is your main takeaway(s) from this lesson? What do you want to take to heart as you go forward?

_____

_____

_____

_____

_____

_____

23. What are some things you will do to apply what you've learned?

_____

_____

_____

_____

_____

_____

Reflect and Respond

"For I know the plans that I have for you," declares the LORD. (Jeremiah 29:11 NASB)

At the end of each lesson you'll find suggested Scripture readings for spending time alone with God during five days of the coming week. Each day of this week's readings will deal with the theme of God calling people to Himself. Read the passage slowly, pausing to think about what is being said. Rather than approaching this as an assignment to complete, think of it as an encounter with a Person. Use any of the questions that are helpful.

Day 1

As He passed by, He saw Levi the son of Alphaeus sitting at the tax office. And He said to him, "Follow Me." So he arose and followed Him. (Mark 2:14)

1. Read Mark 2:13–17. Levi had a successful, though disreputable, job collecting taxes from his fellow Jews on behalf of the Roman government that was occupying his country. What does it say about Jesus that He called such a person to be His disciple?

_____

_____

_____

_____

_____

_____

2. Levi couldn't later change his mind and go back to his old job after walking away from his post. It would have been immediately given to someone else. What did Levi have to believe about Jesus in order to pay this price?

_____

_____

_____

_____

_____

_____

When the scribes and Pharisees saw Him eating with the tax collectors and sinners, they said to His disciples, "How is it that He eats and drinks with tax collectors and sinners?" (Mark 2:16)

3. The Pharisees were appalled that Jesus shared a meal (a sign of relationship) with the least reputable members of their society. Who today would be the equivalent of "tax collectors and sinners" (verse 16)? With whom would your fellow Christians be surprised to see you spending time?

_____

_____

_____

_____

_____

4. What reason did Jesus give for building relationships with tax collectors and sinners? How would you explain this in your own words?

_____
_____
_____
_____
_____

He said to them, "Those who are well have no need of a physician, but those who are sick. I did not come to call the righteous, but sinners, to repentance." (Mark 2:17)

5. When Jesus calls sinners to repentance, does He expect them to change the way they live? What does He ask them to change? What doesn't He ask them to change? (See, for example, Luke 19:1–10.)

_____
_____
_____
_____
_____
_____

Day 2

1. Read Luke 5:1–11. Why does Simon Peter say, "Depart from me, for I am a sinful man, O Lord!" (verse 8)?

_____
_____
_____
_____
_____

When they had done this, they caught a great number of fish. . . . When Simon Peter saw it, he fell down at Jesus' knees, saying, "Depart from me, for I am a sinful man, O Lord!" (Luke 5:6, 8)

2. What does the unexpected catch of fish tell Peter about Jesus?

_____
_____
_____
_____
_____
_____

3. What does Jesus mean when He says, "From now on you will catch men" (verse 10)?

_____
_____
_____
_____
_____

Jesus said to Simon, "Do not be afraid. From now on you will catch men." (Luke 5:10)

4. How has Jesus demonstrated His authority in your life?

_____

_____

_____

5. How has Jesus made you aware of your sinfulness and need of a Savior?

_____

_____

_____

Day 3

Then Elijah passed by him and threw his mantle on him.
(1 Kings 19:19)

1. Read 1 Kings 19:19–21. In this passage, the prophet Elijah calls young Elisha to be trained as his successor. How does Elijah convey this invitation?

_____

_____

_____

_____

[Elisha] said, "Please let me kiss my father and my mother, and then I will follow you."
(1 Kings 19:20)

2. Does it seem okay with Elijah that Elisha wants to say goodbye to his family before leaving them behind to follow Elijah? How do you understand Elijah's words, "Go back again, for what have I done to you?" (verse 20).

_____

_____

_____

_____

3. Elisha has been plowing with twelve pairs of oxen. Most people plowed with just one or two pair, which indicates Elisha came from a prosperous family. How does he celebrate his farewell to his family? What does this say about his decision?

_____

_____

_____

_____

Then he arose and followed Elijah, and became his servant.
(1 Kings 19:21)

4. What aspects of your old life has God asked you to leave behind in your service to Him?

_____

_____

_____

_____

5. What is one area of your life that has been hard to leave behind?

_____

_____

_____

Day 4

1. Read Exodus 3:1–6. What was Moses doing when God called him?

_____

_____

Now Moses was tending the flock of Jethro his father-in-law, the priest of Midian. (Exodus 3:1)

2. How did God get Moses' attention?

_____

_____

_____

3. Why did Moses have to remove his shoes (see verse 5)? What does this say about God?

_____

_____

_____

[God said,] "Take your sandals off your feet, for the place where you stand is holy ground." (Exodus 3:5)

4. Why did Moses hide his face (see verse 6)? What does this say about God?

_____

_____

_____

_____

5. How can you treat God with respect in a manner that is equivalent to removing your shoes in His presence?

_____

_____

_____

_____

The fear of the LORD is a fountain of life. (Proverbs 14:27)

Day 5

1. Read Exodus 3:7–12. What was God calling Moses to do?

_____

_____

_____

Come now, therefore, and I will send you to Pharaoh. (Exodus 3:10)

But Moses said to God, "Who am I that I should go?" (Exodus 3:11)

2. How did Moses respond to God's call (see verse 11)?

_____

_____

_____

_____

_____

"This shall be a sign to you that I have sent you: When you have brought the people out of Egypt, you shall serve God on this mountain." (Exodus 3:12)

3. How did God try to reassure Moses (see verse 12)?

_____

_____

_____

_____

4. Moses made a number of other excuses about serving God (see Exodus 4:1–17). Do you ever make excuses about serving God? If so, what has been one of your excuses?

_____

_____

_____

_____

_____

_____

The LORD came and [called], "Samuel! Samuel!" And Samuel answered, "Speak, for Your servant hears." (1 Samuel 3:10)

5. What is God calling you to now? How are you responding?

_____

_____

_____

_____

_____

Prayer for the Week

Dear Lord, thank You for calling me to Your kingdom and Your service. I know that I'm no better than Levi the tax collector or any other sinner, and it's entirely by your grace that I am a citizen of Your kingdom and a worker in Your vineyard. Your presence is holy ground, and I want to treat that with the greatest respect. How can I serve You? What aspects of my old life do I need to leave behind in order to follow You wholeheartedly? What aspects of my life do You want me to continue in as a mission field? I don't want to make excuses; I want to burn the yoke and cook the oxen and say goodbye to whatever I need to leave behind. Thank You for Your patience with me and Your generous mercy and grace. In our Lord Jesus' name. Amen. ✳

A Lesson About Neighborly Love

And behold, a certain lawyer stood up and tested Him, saying,
"Teacher, what shall I do to inherit eternal life?"

LUKE 10:25

Main Objectives

In this study, you will (1) examine the high standard of perfect love the law sets for those who want to live by it, and (2) consider the depths of the grace of God, who forgives us for falling so far short of His standard.

Read and Review

Read chapter 5 from *Parables* and answer the questions that follow. If you're meeting in a small group, you might want to have someone read each of the following excerpts from *Parables* aloud before you discuss the questions related to it.

A Trick Question

Despite the lawyer's evil motive, the first question he raised is a fine question. It is in fact the greatest question ever asked or answered, and it was frequently on the minds and the hearts of those who approached Jesus to learn from Him. It's what was on the heart of Nicodemus when he came to Jesus under cover of darkness in John 3. It is the very same question the rich young ruler raised in Matthew 19. In fact, that same question was posed frequently to Jesus and appears several places in the Gospels.

Scripture makes a point of noting the man's **insincerity**. This was not an honest question from someone seeking to learn; it was a **test**. (*Parables*, page 77)

This "eternal life" is in essence nothing less than **participation** in the eternal life of the Living Word, **Jesus** Christ. It is the life of God in **every believer**, yet not fully manifest until the resurrection. (*MacArthur Bible Commentary*, page 1359)

The Old Testament promised eternal life, a never-ending kingdom in which true believers would live, in the presence of God, in fulfillment of all the divine promises. Jesus Himself spoke about eternal life often, because that was the central promise of the gospel—the very message He came to proclaim—"that whoever believes in Him should not perish but have everlasting life" (John 3:16). He said things like, "I am the resurrection and the life. He who believes in Me, though he may die, he shall live. And whoever lives and believes in Me shall never die" (John 11:25–26). "Whoever drinks of the water that I shall give him will never thirst. But the water that I shall give him will become in him a fountain of water springing up into everlasting life" (John 4:14). "He who hears My word and believes in Him who sent Me has everlasting life, and shall not come into judgment, but has passed from death into life" (John 5:24)—and so on.

Most Jews had been taught by their rabbis that their lineage, their circumcision, their ceremonies, and their traditions were what qualified them for the eternal kingdom. But clearly there was still a nagging sense of uncertainty and guilt in many hearts, so people constantly raised this question with Jesus. Their own hearts accused them, and they feared that in spite of all their ethnic and religious qualifications, despite what it looked like on the surface, they were only superficially keeping the law and maintaining a front. They knew by the light of conscience that they were not worthy to be a part of that kingdom. (*Parables*, pages 77–78)

And behold, a certain lawyer stood up and tested Him, saying, "Teacher, what shall I do to inherit eternal life?" (Luke 10:25)

1. The "good question" the expert in religious law asked Jesus was, "Teacher, what shall I do to inherit eternal life?" (Luke 10:25). Based on what Jesus said at other times, what would have been a straightforward answer to that question?

_____

_____

_____

_____

_____

_____

But if you want to enter into life, keep the commandments. (Matthew 19:17)

2. Why is this "the greatest question ever asked or answered"?

_____

_____

_____

_____

3. Why did Jesus give a straightforward answer to this question at other times, but not at this time? What clue are we given in Luke 10:25?

_____

_____

_____

_____

_____

A Hard Heart

Jesus was simply holding the mirror of the law up to this legal "expert" to demonstrate how the law condemned him. If the lawyer were an honest man, he ought to have acknowledged that he did not love God as he should; he didn't even love his neighbors as he should. This man, steeped in the study of God's law, should have been broken by the law's message. He should have felt deep conviction. He should have been penitent, contrite, humble. His follow-up question ought to have been something like this: "I know from bitter experience that I cannot fulfill even the most basic commandments of the law; where can I find redemption?"

*Instead, he doused the fire of his conscience with the water of self-righteous pride. "But he, **wanting to justify himself**, said to Jesus, 'And who is my neighbor?'" (Luke 10:29, emphasis added).*

He wanted to convince people that he was righteous, although he knew he wasn't. He wanted to maintain the facade. This was the whole problem with the legalists, Pharisees, and other self-righteous religious bullies who constantly challenged Jesus. They "trusted in themselves that they were righteous, and despised others" (Luke 18:9). It was Jesus' central criticism of the Pharisees' brand of religion. He told them, "You are those who justify yourselves before men, but God knows your hearts" (Luke 16:15). In the words of the apostle Paul, "They being ignorant of God's righteousness, and seeking to establish their own righteousness, [did not submit] to the righteousness of God" (Romans 10:3). This particular legalist was desperate to make himself look good in others' eyes, regardless of what God thought of him. (Parables, pages 79–80)

4. When Jesus said to the expert in the law, "Do this [love God with all your being and your neighbor as yourself] and you will live," why would the appropriate response on the man's part have been humility and penitence?

_____

_____

_____

_____

5. Why is this kind of humility so hard for some people?

_____

_____

_____

6. How was the legal expert in Luke 10:25–28 "ignorant of God's righteousness" (Romans 10:3)? What did he not understand about God's righteousness?

_____

_____

_____

_____

Law: An inward principle of action, either good or evil, operating with the regularity of a law. The term also designates a standard for a person's life. . . . God's law is the standard for human action that corresponds to the righteous nature of God. (*MacArthur Bible Commentary*, page 1526)

If anyone thinks himself to be something, when he is nothing, he deceives himself. (Galatians 6:3)

Let nothing be done through selfish ambition or conceit, but in lowliness of mind let each esteem others better than himself. (Philippians 2:3)

The Priest and the Levite

Priest: A servant of God, one who offers sacrifices for people in the temple. (*Parables*, page 83)

It's right, of course, to condemn the callous disregard of these two men [the priest and the Levite] and look upon their deliberate heedlessness with utter scorn. But in doing so, we condemn ourselves as well. Their attitude is precisely what we see in human nature today, even within our own hearts. We think, "I don't want to get involved. I don't know what this man, or the people who beat him up, might do to me." Without in any way justifying the coldhearted apathy Jesus was condemning, we must confess that we, too, are guilty of similar blind indifference, wretched insensitivity, and careless disregard of people in dire need. Even if we don't turn away every time we see someone in need, we all fail in this duty enough to stand guilty before the law with its demand for utter perfection. (Parables, page 86)

Levite: Descendants of Levi [who] . . . served in subordinate roles in the temple. (*Parables*, page 85)

7. Think of an opportunity you had to show compassion for someone you didn't know. Maybe you saw a homeless person by the side of the road, or someone in your church was in need, or you heard about people suffering from poverty or a natural disaster. What did you do?

_____

_____

_____

_____

8. What thought process led you to do what you did?

_____

_____

_____

_____

Compassion: Sympathetic consciousness of others' distress together with a desire to alleviate it. (*Merriam-Webster*)

9. What for you are the biggest obstacles to consistent compassion for those in need?

_____

_____

_____

_____

Make the Connection

Read the following Scripture passages and answer the questions provided. If you are meeting in a small group, you might want to have someone read each passage aloud before you discuss the questions related to it.

And behold, a certain lawyer stood up and tested Him, saying, "Teacher, what shall I do to inherit eternal life?"

He said to him, "What is written in the law? What is your reading of it?"

So he answered and said, "'You shall love the Lord your God with all your heart, with all your soul, with all your strength, and with all your mind,' and 'your neighbor as yourself.'"

And He said to him, "You have answered rightly; do this and you will live."

But he, wanting to justify himself, said to Jesus, "And who is my neighbor?"

Then Jesus answered and said: "A certain man went down from Jerusalem to Jericho, and fell among thieves, who stripped him of his clothing, wounded him, and departed, leaving him half dead. Now by chance a certain priest came down that road. And when he saw him, he passed by on the other side. Likewise a Levite, when he arrived at the place, came and looked, and passed by on the other side. But a certain Samaritan, as he journeyed, came where he was. And when he saw him, he had compassion. So he went to him and bandaged his wounds, pouring on oil and wine; and he set him on his own animal, brought him to an inn, and took care of him. On the next day, when he departed, he took out two denarii, gave them to the innkeeper, and said to him, 'Take care of him; and whatever more you spend, when I come again, I will repay you.' So which of these three do you think was neighbor to him who fell among the thieves?"

And he said, "He who showed mercy on him."

Then Jesus said to him, "Go and do likewise." (Luke 10:25–37)

The prevailing opinion among **scribes** and **Pharisees** was that one's neighbors were the righteous alone. According to them, the **wicked**—including rank sinners (such as tax collectors and prostitutes), Gentiles, and especially **Samaritans**—were to be hated because they were the **enemies** of God. (*MacArthur Bible Commentary*, page 1298)

For a Samaritan to travel this road was **unusual**. The Samaritan himself was risking not only the **thieves**, but also the hostility of other **travelers**. (*MacArthur Bible Commentary*, page 1299)

10. How does Jesus' story answer the question, "Who is my neighbor?"

_____

_____

_____

_____

11. What standard does Jesus' story set for loving our neighbor enough to satisfy God's law?

_____

_____

_____

_____

12. What would be a good response to hearing the story and then being told, "Go and do likewise"?

Let your light so shine before men, that they may see your good works and glorify your Father. (Matthew 5:16)

_____

_____

_____

_____

_____

These verses plainly teach that God's love extends even to His **enemies**. . . . It must be distinguished from the everlasting **love** God has for the elect, but it is a sincere **goodwill** nonetheless. (*MacArthur Bible Commentary*, page 1132)

[Jesus said,] "You have heard that it was said, 'You shall love your neighbor and hate your enemy.' But I say to you, love your enemies, bless those who curse you, do good to those who hate you, and pray for those who spitefully use you and persecute you, that you may be sons of your Father in heaven; for He makes His sun rise on the evil and on the good, and sends rain on the just and on the unjust. For if you love those who love you, what reward have you? Do not even the tax collectors do the same? And if you greet your brethren only, what do you do more than others? Do not even the tax collectors do so? Therefore you shall be perfect, just as your Father in heaven is perfect."* (Matthew 5:43–48)

13. What standard of behavior does Jesus set in this excerpt from the Sermon on the Mount?

_____

_____

_____

_____

_____

14. Do you think Jesus actually expects us to take Him at His word and try to do this? Or is He just trying to set an impossible standard so we know how hard it would be to live by the law and how much we need grace?

_____

_____

_____

_____

_____

_____

Walk in love, as Christ also has loved us and given Himself for us, an offering and a sacrifice to God. (Ephesians 5:2)

15. Have you ever tried to love an enemy or someone who hated you? If so, what happened?

_____

_____

_____

_____

_____

Explore the Key Points

Take some time to consider how some of the big ideas of this chapter intersect with your own life. It will be helpful to answer these questions on your own before you discuss them with your group. If you're meeting with a group, you may want to have someone read aloud the key point before you discuss it.

Love Like the Samaritan

Like the priest and the Levite, the Samaritan saw the wounded man. But unlike them, he was moved with grief and empathy. He embraced the urgent need to rescue the man. *He bore the injured man's burden as if it were his own.*

The Samaritan used his own wine and oil to disinfect and soothe the man's wounds. He poured them out generously. Then he set the man on his own donkey or mule, and he walked to the nearest inn while the wounded man rode. At the inn, he took care of the man, providing food, water, and whatever other care the injured man needed. He didn't leave the man until the next day, and even then he paid the innkeeper enough money for two months' room and board. He even promised to pay more if the bill exceeded that amount. He gave up his own supplies, his time, a night's sleep, and a significant sum of cash for a complete stranger from an enemy ethnic group.

This is what it means to love our neighbor as ourselves. The Samaritan didn't stop to wrestle with whether he wanted to get involved. Rather, he did what he would have done for himself, sparing no expense. This is God's commandment, and we are called to develop profound compassion for the people we encounter—even strangers.

If we're honest, however, we'll admit we fall far short of this standard. Often we're like the priest and Levite, not wanting to get involved. If we do reach out and help someone, we seldom do it with this level of total abandon unless the person is a close friend or family member. That's why we can be overjoyed that God offers us mercy and grace for falling short of His standard in this area. We should be more compassionate than we are. By God's grace we *can* become more compassionate than we are. And by God's grace we are forgiven for being only as compassionate as we are.

16. What aspect of the Samaritan's care for the injured man most surprises you? In what area do you feel he most went above and beyond?

_____

_____

_____

_____

_____

_____

17. What opportunities for showing compassion to others do you currently have? What will that cost you?

_____

_____

_____

_____

_____

_____

In Jesus' time, animosity between **Jews** and **Samaritans** was especially fierce. The depth of the Jews' **contempt** for their wayward cousins is seen not only in how they avoided **traveling** through Samaria, but perhaps even more in how they **spoke** about the Samaritans. (*Parables*, page 88)

You shall not take vengeance, nor bear any grudge against the children of your people, but you shall love your neighbor as yourself. (Leviticus 19:18)

Do not forget to entertain strangers, for by so doing some have unwittingly entertained angels. (Hebrews 13:2)

18. Think of the level of compassion you have shown others during the past year. Does that reflection move you more to be proud of yourself or more to be grateful for God's grace? Why?

_____

_____

_____

_____

God's Love for Sinners

I pray that you . . . grasp how wide and long and high and deep is the love of Christ.
(Ephesians 3:17–18 NIV)

The way the good Samaritan cared for the traveler is the way God loves sinners. In fact, God's love is infinitely more profound and amazing than the Samaritan's care. The Samaritan sacrificed his time and money to care for a wounded enemy. But God gave His own Son to die for sinners who deserved nothing more than eternal damnation.

As Paul wrote, "When we were still without strength, in due time Christ died for the ungodly. For scarcely for a righteous man will one die; yet perhaps for a good man someone would even dare to die. But God demonstrates His own love toward us, in that while we were still sinners, Christ died for us" (Romans 5:6–8). Indeed, "when we were *enemies* we were reconciled to God through the death of His Son" (verse 10, emphasis added).

*If that lawyer had truly looked into the **law** of God . . . he would have found a **Savior** whose yoke is easy and whose burden is light.*
(*Parables*, pages 93–94)

If the lawyer had just confessed his guilt and admitted his inability to do what the law demanded, Jesus would have been ready to offer him an eternity of mercy, grace, and forgiveness. The straightforward answer to the man's question was already on the lips of Jesus, who repeatedly said things such as, "He who hears My word and believes in Him who sent Me has everlasting life, and shall not come into judgment, but has passed from death into life" (John 5:24); "He who believes in the Son has everlasting life" (3:36); "My sheep hear My voice, and I know them . . . I give them eternal life, and they shall never perish" (10:27–28); and, "Whoever lives and believes in Me shall never die" (11:26).

19. How have you experienced God's love when you were in danger or in need?

_____

_____

_____

When [Jesus] saw the multitudes, He was moved with compassion.
(Matthew 9:36)

20. How are you moved to respond to God's love? Are you moved to acts of compassion, acts of worship, or something else?

_____

_____

_____

21. When you think about your own inability to do what the law requires, how deeply does that affect you? Do you feel guilt, humility, repentance? Or do you tend to think, *Of course I can't live up to that standard, and it's no big deal*? Explain.

_____

_____

_____

_____

_____

_____

Those who forsake the law praise the wicked, but such as keep the law contend with them. (Proverbs 28:4)

Living the Parable

We've covered a lot in this lesson. Now it is your chance to pull it all together and decide what is the most important principle(s) you need to take to heart. You probably can't change your life in half a dozen ways this week, so prayerfully consider what is God's top priority for you.

22. What is your main takeaway(s) from this lesson? What do you want to take to heart as you go forward?

_____

_____

_____

_____

_____

_____

_____

23. What are some things you will do to apply what you've learned?

_____

_____

_____

_____

_____

_____

Reflect and Respond

At the end of each lesson, you will find suggested Scripture readings for spending time alone with God during five days of the coming week. Each day of this week's readings will deal with the theme of loving others because God has loved us. Read each passage slowly, pausing to think about what is being said. Rather than approaching this as an assignment

God's love (*agape*): Respect, devotion, and affection that leads to willing, self-sacrificial service. (*MacArthur Bible Commentary*, page 1676)

to complete, think of it as an encounter with your heavenly Father. Use any of the questions that are helpful.

Day 1

1. Read Romans 12:9–13. In these verses, Paul lists some of the things his readers should do in response to receiving God's grace and mercy. Why is it important to pursue such actions as a response to grace rather than a way of *earning* God's approval?

_____

_____

_____

_____

_____

Let love be without hypocrisy. Abhor what is evil. Cling to what is good. (Romans 12:9)

2. Paul says, "Let love be without hypocrisy" (verse 9). How would you explain what he means in your own words? Give an example of hypocrisy-free love.

_____

_____

_____

_____

_____

Be kindly affectionate to one another with brotherly love . . . distributing to the needs of the saints, given to hospitality. (Romans 12:10, 13)

3. Why is "distributing to the needs of the saints" (verse 13) an important form of love? What might this look like in our day?

_____

_____

_____

_____

_____

4. What is hospitality? How is it different from simply entertaining people? How can it be a form of love?

_____

_____

_____

_____

_____

5. Which of Paul's exhortations do you find fairly easy to follow? Which ones do you need extra grace to pursue?

_____

_____

_____

_____

_____

Day 2

1. Read Romans 12:14–21. How does Paul want us to treat people who try to harm us?

_____

_____

_____

_____

Bless those who persecute you; bless and do not curse. Rejoice with those who rejoice, and weep with those who weep. Be of the same mind toward one another. (Romans 12:14–16)

2. What is the reasoning behind his counsel? Do you think he is being realistic? Why or why not?

_____

_____

_____

_____

3. How easy or hard is it for you to practice these instructions? Is this an area where you need grace? Explain.

_____

_____

_____

_____

4. Do you tend to live peaceably with people, or do you tend to have a fair amount of conflict? Why do you think that's the case?

_____

_____

_____

_____

If it is possible, as much as depends on you, live peaceably with all men. (Romans 12:18)

5. Why is weeping "with those who weep" (verse 15) an important aspect of love?

_____

_____

_____

_____

Day 3

1. Read Galatians 5:13–16. What might it look like to use Christian liberty "as an opportunity for the flesh" (verse 13)? Give an example.

_____

_____

_____

Do not use liberty as an opportunity for the flesh, but through love serve one another. (Galatians 5:13)

2. What does it look like to exercise Christian liberty without indulging the flesh? Give an example.

_____
_____
_____
_____

3. When Paul says that loving our neighbor fulfills the law, is he saying we don't need to practice it because we're under grace? Explain.

_____
_____
_____
_____

4. Does liberty spur you on to love? Why or why not?

_____
_____
_____
_____

5. What does it mean to "walk in the Spirit" (verse 16)? How does a person go about doing that?

_____
_____
_____
_____

Day 4

1. Read 1 John 3:10–12, 16–18. According to verse 10, how can we tell the difference between people who are children of God and people who aren't?

_____
_____
_____
_____
_____

2. Is John talking about earning our place as children of God? Where do you see the gospel of grace in his words?

_____
_____
_____
_____

3. What does it mean to lay down our lives for our brothers and sisters in Christ? Give an example.

_____

_____

_____

_____

By this we know love, because He laid down His life for us. And we also ought to lay down our lives for the brethren. (1 John 3:16)

4. What does it mean to love in deed and in truth, not just in words?

_____

_____

_____

_____

Let us not love in word or in tongue, but in deed and in truth. (1 John 3:18)

5. We know that we can never live up to this standard perfectly. However, what do you believe you are being called to do to love others today?

_____

_____

_____

_____

_____

Day 5

1. Read 1 John 4:7–11. What reasons for loving others does John give

_____

_____

_____

_____

Beloved, let us love one another, for love is of God. (1 John 4:1)

2. Where is the grace of God in this passage?

_____

_____

_____

_____

3. What does it mean to say that "God is love" (verse 8)? How is this different from saying that love is God?

_____

_____

_____

_____

_____

He who does not love does not know God, for God is love. (1 John 4:8)

In this the love of God was manifested toward us, that God has sent His only begotten Son.
(1 John 4:9)

4. How has God demonstrated His love for you?

_____

_____

_____

_____

_____

_____

Beloved, if God so loved us, we also ought to love one another.
(1 John 4:11)

5. What opportunity for love do you have today? What grace do you need to do that?

_____

_____

_____

_____

_____

_____

Prayer for the Week

Dear Lord, thank You for offering me abundant forgiveness when I fall short of Your standard of love. Thank You for providing me with the grace of the indwelling Holy Spirit to help me grow in love. I am indescribably grateful that Your blood covers my deep limitations and my sinful weakness in all my attempts to love. There is no way I can love as well as You have loved me, laying down Your life for me, and yet I know You call me to take small steps in that direction for the people you have placed in my life. I can't possibly earn Your approval through love, but I can respond to Your gift of grace through love, and today I ask You to empower me through Your Spirit to do that. Show me opportunities to love this week. In our Lord Jesus' name. Amen. ❋

A Lesson About
Justification by Faith

*He spoke this parable to some who trusted in themselves
that they were righteous, and despised others.*

LUKE 18:9

Main Objectives

In this study, you will (1) look at what "justification by faith" means and what its implications are for us, and (2) consider issues of pride in our lives and how we can grow in humility.

Read and Review

Read chapter 6 from *Parables* and answer the questions that follow. If you're meeting in a small group, you might want to have someone read each of the following excerpts from *Parables* aloud before you discuss the questions related to it.

The Problem for Sinners

It is easy to see why the justification of sinners posed an impossible dilemma for people prior to the death and resurrection of Christ.... The difficulty starts with an understanding of the law's righteous requirement. In Leviticus 19:2, God Himself says, "You shall be holy, for I the LORD your God am holy." God's own perfect holiness therefore establishes the legal standard and the moral requirement for a right standing with God. Jesus reiterates that same standard in the New Testament, this

Holy: Worthy of complete devotion as one perfect in goodness and righteousness. (*Merriam-Webster*)

71

[The Pharisees] used the **law** to disguise what was really in their **hearts**—and they salved their own guilt by **self-righteously** comparing themselves with others. (*Parables*, pages 99–100)

The marvelous truth of the **gospel** is that **Christ** has met this standard [of perfection] on our **behalf**. (*MacArthur Bible Commentary*, page 1132)

For whoever shall keep the whole law, and yet stumble in one point, he is guilty of all. (James 2:10)

I say to you that whoever is angry with his brother without a cause shall be in danger of the judgment. (Matthew 5:22)

time with language clearly designed to stress the sheer impossibility of attaining such a high standard. In His Sermon on the Mount, He said, "Unless your righteousness exceeds the righteousness of the scribes and Pharisees, you will by no means enter the kingdom of heaven" (Matthew 5:20).

That was undoubtedly a major shock to everyone who heard it. Say what you will about the Pharisees' hypocrisy and hidden wickedness, they had nevertheless elevated obedience to the law's external commands to an unprecedented level. If God graded human behavior on a curve, the Pharisees would have been at the head of the class. But Jesus was pointing out that God doesn't adjust the scale of righteousness to accommodate human failure. His own righteousness is flawlessly perfect, and to lower that standard even slightly in order to accommodate our sin would make Him unholy.

So the righteousness God demands must exceed even the apparently superior righteousness of the Pharisees. What, precisely, does this require of us? Jesus answers that question, too, and in unequivocal terms: "You shall be perfect, just as your Father in heaven is perfect" (Matthew 5:48). True righteousness, as defined by the character of God Himself, demands absolute, uncompromising perfection. He Himself is the standard and only true measure of the perfection He requires from us. (Parables, pages 103–104)

1. Why does God require absolute moral perfection from human beings? Why doesn't He grade on a curve?

_____

_____

_____

_____

_____

2. In what ways does it surprise you that God has a standard for us of absolute holiness? In what ways does it seem unfair? Explain.

_____

_____

_____

_____

3. Read Matthew 5:21–22, 27–30. How does Jesus make clear that the standard of God's law is even higher than the Pharisees believed?

_____

_____

_____

_____

Imputed Righteousness

*Who, then, can be right with God? If God says it is evil to justify anyone who is guilty, and He states emphatically that He will not justify the wicked, how can anyone who has ever sinned be granted entry into the heavenly kingdom? The answer is hinted at in the Genesis record of Abraham: "He believed in the LORD; and He reckoned it to him as righteousness" (Genesis 15:6 NASB). Righteousness was **imputed** to Abraham. A righteousness that did not belong to him was credited to his account (Romans 4:1–12). He did not earn righteousness by his works; he laid hold of it by faith. Furthermore, "[all] those who are of faith are blessed with Abraham, the believer" (Galatians 3:9 NASB). That is the doctrine of justification by faith.*

But on what grounds is such justification possible, given that God says He will not simply acquit sinners or declare them righteous by divine fiat alone?

The full answer to that question is seen in the sacrifice offered by Jesus Christ. God does not dismiss the guilt of sinners by pretending their sin never happened. He doesn't ignore evil, sweep it aside by sheer edict, or acquit sinners capriciously on a whim. Rather, He provided a full and perfect atonement for sin in the Person of His own Son, "whom God set forth as a propitiation by His blood, through faith, to demonstrate His righteousness" (Romans 3:25). Christ also provides the perfect righteousness that is imputed to those who believe: "[God the Father] made Him who knew no sin to be sin on our behalf, so that we might become the righteousness of God in Him" (2 Corinthians 5:21 NASB). (Parables, pages 104–105)

4. What does *imputed* mean? What does it mean to have righteousness imputed to us?

_____

_____

_____

_____

_____

_____

_____

5. Is faith an action by which we earn Jesus' righteousness? Explain.

_____

_____

_____

_____

_____

6. What does *atonement* mean? What does it mean that Jesus atoned for our sin?

_____

_____

_____

_____

_____

Justification: When we believe in Jesus, God imputes His righteousness to us, and we are declared righteous before God. (*MacArthur Bible Commentary*, page 1516)

Jesus' message is simple: all who are determined to establish a **righteousness** of their own will fail and thus **condemn** themselves; but those who **submit** to the righteousness of God are graciously **justified** by Him. (*Parables*, page 107)

He chose us in Him before the foundation of the world, that we should be holy and without blame before Him in love. (Ephesians 1:4)

[Jesus] bore our sins in His own body on the tree, that we, having died to sins, might live for righteousness. (1 Peter 2:24)

The **only thing** the Pharisee really had in great abundance was a surplus of **self-esteem**. He clearly thought more highly of himself than he **ought** to think. This is where the contrast between him and the tax collector is most clearly **evident**. (*Parables*, page 115)

Similar Beliefs

*The Pharisee and the tax collector actually held many of their core beliefs in common. . . . The Pharisee **did** believe in the need for atonement. No one with a Pharisee's knowledge of the law could possibly believe he was totally sinless. But he thought he had earned the right to be forgiven. In other words, he believed he had effectively atoned for his own sins. He apparently thought his good works outweighed and nullified his failures. He had offered the requisite sacrifices. He had performed so much better than most. Surely if good works and religious devotion could tip the scales of divine justice in one's own favor, this Pharisee of all people deserved a place of high honor. That's the way most religious people think. Most aren't the least bit reluctant to confess that they have sinned; they just can't seem to come to grips with the fact that their good works cannot earn them any merit. They think God is going to forgive the bad things they have done because they have earned His favor with good works.*

The tax collector may have thought that way once, too, but life had brought him to the realization that he had nothing with which to bargain for God's favor. His very best deeds were defiled by the now obvious truth of who he really was at heart. The lesson of Isaiah 64:6 had been thrust upon him in living color: "We are all like an unclean thing, and all our righteousnesses are like filthy rags."

*The misery he must have felt on coming to that understanding was actually a gracious gift from God—the necessary precursor to the man's redemption. "Godly sorrow produces repentance leading to salvation, not to be regretted" (2 Corinthians 7:10). (*Parables*, pages 115–116)*

A man is not justified by the works of the law but by faith in Jesus. (Galatians 2:16)

7. How did temple sacrifices for atonement fit into the Pharisee's belief system?

_____

_____

_____

_____

_____

8. Do you know people who believe the good they do outweighs the bad? If so, what do they expect will happen to them when they die? Why do they think that?

_____

_____

_____

_____

_____

Draw near to God and He will draw near to you. (James 4:8)

9. Why was the tax collector's misery a good thing for him?

_____

_____

_____

_____

_____

Make the Connection

Read the following Scripture passages and answer the questions provided. If you are meeting in a small group, you might want to have someone read each passage aloud before you discuss the questions related to it.

> *He spoke this parable to some who trusted in themselves that they were righteous, and despised others: "Two men went up to the temple to pray, one a Pharisee and the other a tax collector. The Pharisee stood and prayed thus with himself, 'God, I thank You that I am not like other men—extortioners, unjust, adulterers, or even as this tax collector. I fast twice a week; I give tithes of all that I possess.' And the tax collector, standing afar off, would not so much as raise his eyes to heaven, but beat his breast, saying, 'God, be merciful to me a sinner!' I tell you, this man went down to his house justified rather than the other; for everyone who exalts himself will be humbled, and he who humbles himself will be exalted." (Luke 18:9–14)*

This parable . . . illustrates perfectly how a **sinner** who is utterly devoid of personal **righteousness** may be declared righteous before God instantaneously through an act of **repentant faith.** (*MacArthur Bible Commentary,* page 1316)

10. How does the Pharisee exalt himself?

_____

_____

_____

_____

_____

11. How does the tax collector humble himself?

_____

_____

_____

[The tax collector] had no **hope** but the **mercy** of God. This is the point to which the law aims to bring **every** sinner. (*MacArthur Bible Commentary,* page 1316)

12. How does this passage teach the doctrine of justification by faith alone, apart from works?

_____

_____

_____

_____

_____

> *Surely He has borne our griefs*
> *And carried our sorrows;*
> *Yet we esteemed Him stricken,*
> *Smitten by God, and afflicted.*
> *But He was wounded for our transgressions,*
> *He was bruised for our iniquities;*

[Jesus] was delivered up because of our offenses, and was raised because of our justification. (Romans 4:25)

[Jesus] **suffered** the chastisement of God in order to procure the believer's **peace** with God. The stripe . . . that caused His death has brought **salvation** to those for whose sins He died. (*MacArthur Bible Commentary*, page 828)

The Servant lost His life to be the **substitute** object of wrath in the place of the Jews, who by that substitution will receive **salvation** and the righteousness of God **imputed** to them. (*MacArthur Bible Commentary*, page 828)

The chastisement for our peace was upon Him,
And by His stripes we are healed.
All we like sheep have gone astray;
We have turned, every one, to his own way;
And the LORD has laid on Him the iniquity of us all.

He was oppressed and He was afflicted,
Yet He opened not His mouth;
He was led as a lamb to the slaughter,
And as a sheep before its shearers is silent,
So He opened not His mouth.
He was taken from prison and from judgment,
And who will declare His generation?
For He was cut off from the land of the living;
For the transgressions of My people He was stricken.
And they made His grave with the wicked—
But with the rich at His death,
Because He had done no violence,
Nor was any deceit in His mouth.

Yet it pleased the Lord to bruise Him;
He has put Him to grief.
When You make His soul an offering for sin,
He shall see His seed, He shall prolong His days,
And the pleasure of the Lord shall prosper in His hand.
He shall see the labor of His soul, and be satisfied.
By His knowledge My righteous Servant shall justify many,
For He shall bear their iniquities. (Isaiah 53:4–11)

13. This prophecy in Isaiah 53 predicted Jesus' sacrifice for sin centuries before it occurred. Where in this passage do you see a prediction of Jesus paying the price for our sin so we could have His righteousness imputed to us?

_____

_____

_____

_____

_____

[David], foreseeing this, spoke concerning the resurrection of the Christ, that His soul was not left in Hades, nor did His flesh see corruption. (Acts 2:31)

14. What can we learn about God from the fact that Jesus' sacrifice was predicted centuries before it happened?

_____

_____

_____

_____

15. What does this part of the passage predict: "When You make His soul an offering for sin, He shall see His seed, He shall prolong His days, and the pleasure of the Lord shall prosper in His hand. He shall see the labor of His soul, and be satisfied"?

_____

_____

_____

_____

_____

_____

Purge out the old leaven . . . since you truly are unleavened. For indeed Christ, our Passover, was sacrificed for us. (1 Corinthians 5:5)

Explore the Key Points

Take some time to consider how some of the big ideas of this chapter intersect with your own life. It will be helpful to answer these questions on your own before you discuss them with your group. If you're meeting with a group, you may want to have someone read aloud the key point before you discuss it.

Pharisees and the Gospel

Jesus criticized the beliefs of the Pharisees not because they represented the worst perversion of religion but because they were such a subtle perversion of true religion. The Pharisees were far closer to Jesus' teaching than were the pagan Romans, or even than the priests who ran the temple in Jerusalem. The Pharisees at least took God's law seriously and tried to keep it. We need to grapple with these faulty beliefs not because they are the worst error we could fall into but because thay are common errors to which we can easily succumb.

Woe to you, scribes and Pharisees, hypocrites! For you are like whitewashed tombs which indeed appear beautiful outwardly, but inside are full of dead men's bones and all uncleanness. (Matthew 23:27)

The Pharisees were concerned with the purity of laypeople. In fact, they were so concerned that ordinary Jews would be corrupted by contact with idolatrous pagans that they constructed a code by which ordinary Jews could keep themselves outwardly pure and separate from idolatry. The Pharisees even adapted some of the laws regarding purity for priests and applied them to laypeople. By following these laws, they believed laypeople could be as pure as the priests serving in the temple were supposed to be.

Tragically, this emphasis on purity and scrupulous observance of laws such as the tithe and the Sabbath distracted the Pharisees from laws that were much harder to keep, such as the commandment not to covet and the command to love one's neighbor as oneself. They tended to define those laws narrowly so they could claim to keep them. Their system blinded them to their guilt in matters such as greed, deceit, malice, and contempt for those outside their circle.

What the law could not do in that it was weak through the flesh, God did by sending His own Son in the likeness of sinful flesh. (Romans 8:3)

Pride goes before destruction, and a haughty spirit before a fall.
(Proverbs 16:18)

Jesus tried in vain to show the Pharisees their hearts, but His efforts only cemented their hatred of Him. Their central sin was pride—the belief they could perform well enough in the law's external details that they could please God. They didn't understand the law was intended to humble them by showing them the magnitude of their guilt and need for atonement.

16. In what ways is the sin of the Pharisees a greater temptation for professing Christians than outright idolatry?

_____

_____

_____

_____

_____

*Jesus' **point** is crystal clear. He was teaching that justification is by **faith alone.***
(*Parables*, page 118)

17. Have you ever been tempted to trust in the external observance of the "rules" of Christianity? If so, what was that like for you? If not, what has kept you free of that temptation?

_____

_____

_____

_____

_____

_____

18. What is it about pride that makes it such a deadly, damnable sin?

_____

_____

_____

_____

_____

The Tax Collector and the Gospel

Tax collectors made their money by agreeing to pay a fixed amount to the Romans each year and then extorting an extra percentage from the taxpayers. Chief tax collectors tended to become rich because they were good at taking advantage of their fellow Jews. They were, therefore, generally hated by the Jews and excluded from society.

[Jesus] saw a man named Matthew sitting at the tax office. And He said to him, "Follow Me." So he arose and followed Him.
(Matthew 9:9)

When Jesus called Matthew to be His disciple, Matthew left his toll collector's booth and followed Him (see Matthew 9:9). The implication was that Matthew abandoned his corrupt career to travel with Jesus. Likewise, after Jesus dined at the home of Zacchaeus, a chief tax collector, Zacchaeus said, "Look, Lord, I give half of my goods to the poor; and if I have taken anything from anyone by false accusation, I restore fourfold" (Luke 19:8). These two tax collectors took action that reflected true repentance.

In Jesus' parable, however, we don't see the tax collector promising to quit his job or restore his ill-gotten gains to their rightful owners. Instead, the signs of repentance we see are his standing far from God's holy place in the temple, his unwillingness to lift his eyes to heaven, his beating of his breast with grief over his sin, and his begging for mercy. Here, the emphasis is on the fact that this man needed to do no good work to merit his justification. His pure repentance and faith were everything. The fruit of repentance could come later. He went away fully justified without performing any works of penance, without doing any sacrament or ritual, without any meritorious works whatsoever.

True gospel ministry points sinners to repentance. It's not sufficient to tell sinners that God loves them and has a wonderful plan for their lives. Before the gospel can come as truly good news, the sinner must come to grips with the bad news of the law. This tax collector came to grips with that, and this is what drove him to repentance.

> Here was a man who had been made to face the **reality** of his own sin, and his only response was abject **humility** and **repentance**. (*MacArthur Bible Commentary*, page 1317)

> **Gospel:** Literally "good news" or "good message" . . . the good news of salvation. (*MacArthur Bible Commentary*, page 1194)

19. The tax collector looked to God to do for him what he couldn't do for himself: atone for his sin. How easy is it for you to be in that place of acknowledging your helplessness to atone for what you've done? Do you tend to feel there should be something you can do? Or do you tend to like the feeling that nothing is expected of you?

20. Would God still forgive the tax collector if he returned to his corrupt job after this episode of penitence? Explain.

21. Who are the "tax collectors"—the people who seem least likely to repent—in your world? How are you moved to pray for them?

> *I exhort first of all that supplications, prayers, intercessions, and giving of thanks be made for all men.* (1 Timothy 2:1)

Living the Parable

We've covered a lot in this lesson. Now it is your chance to pull it all together and decide what is the most important principle(s) you need to take to heart. You probably can't change your life in half a dozen ways this week, so prayerfully consider what is God's top priority for you.

22. What is your main takeaway(s) from this lesson? What do you want to take to heart as you go forward?

_____

_____

_____

_____

_____

23. What are some things you will do to apply what you've learned?

_____

_____

_____

_____

_____

Reflect and Respond

Only **God** is truly exalted, and therefore only God can **exalt** men. He does this by conferring on them the perfect **righteousness** of Christ.
(*Parables*, page 120)

At the end of each lesson, you will find suggested Scripture readings for spending time alone with God during five days of the coming week. Each day of this week's readings will deal with the theme of justification by faith. Read each passage slowly, pausing to think about what is being said. Rather than approaching this as an assignment to complete, think of it as an encounter with your heavenly Father. Use any of the questions that are helpful.

Day 1

When the kindness and the love of God our Savior toward man appeared, not by works of righteousness which we have done.
(Titus 3:4–5)

1. Read Titus 3:4–7. How does Paul articulate the idea that we are justified solely by God's grace and not by our works?

_____

_____

_____

_____

_____

_____

2. What is the Holy Spirit's role in our justification?

_____

_____

_____

_____

_____

_____

According to His mercy He saved us, through the washing of regeneration and renewing of the Holy Spirit, whom He poured out on us abundantly through Jesus Christ. (Titus 3:5–6)

3. Why is it important that the Spirit has been poured out "abundantly" (verse 6)?

_____

_____

_____

_____

_____

_____

4. Why does Paul call us "heirs" (verse 7)? What do we inherit?

_____

_____

_____

_____

_____

Having been justified by His grace we should become heirs according to the hope of eternal life. (Titus 3:7)

5. Is this good news to you personally? Why or why not?

_____

_____

_____

_____

_____

Day 2

1. Read Genesis 15:1–6. What did God want Abraham to believe in verse 1?

_____

_____

_____

_____

The word of the LORD came to Abram . . . saying, "Do not be afraid, Abram. I am your shield, your exceedingly great reward." But Abram said, "Lord GOD, what will You give me, seeing I go childless, and the heir of my house is Eliezer of Damascus?" (Genesis 15:1–2)

2. What moved Abraham to question whether God truly was who He said He was (see verses 2–3; see also Genesis 12:2)?

_____

_____

_____

_____

[God] brought [Abram] outside and said, "Look now toward heaven, and count the stars if you are able to number them." And He said to him, "So shall your descendants be." And he believed in the LORD, and He accounted it to him for righteousness.
(Genesis 15:5–6)

3. What did God promise Abraham (see verses 4–5)?

_____

_____

_____

_____

4. Abraham was far from a perfect man. So why did God credit him as being righteous (see verse 6)? What did Abraham believe?

_____

_____

_____

_____

_____

For if Abraham was justified by works, he has something to boast about, but not before God.
(Romans 4:2)

5. Think about your own situation. What do you have to believe in order to be credited as righteous? How is your situation like and unlike Abraham's?

_____

_____

_____

_____

_____

_____

_____

Day 3

By the deeds of the law no flesh will be justified in His sight, for by the law is the knowledge of sin.
(Romans 3:20)

1. Read Romans 3:20–26. According to Paul, the purpose of the law is to bring "the knowledge of sin" (verse 20). Explain in your own words what this means.

_____

_____

_____

_____

_____

2. In what ways has God's law served that purpose in your life? Explain.

_____

_____

_____

_____

_____

3. Paul says righteousness comes through faith in Jesus Christ (see verse 22). What does it mean to have faith in Christ? Why is it more than simply a matter of believing certain facts about Christ?

_____

_____

_____

_____

_____

_____

The righteousness of God apart from the law is revealed, being witnessed by the Law and the Prophets, even the righteousness of God, through faith in Jesus Christ. (Romans 3:21–22)

4. Paul says God set forth Christ "as a propitiation by His blood" (verse 25). What does that mean to you? What is *propitiation*?

_____

_____

_____

_____

_____

_____

5. How have you needed propitiation by Christ's blood? How are you moved to respond to having received this propitiation?

_____

_____

_____

_____

_____

_____

_____

God set forth [Jesus] as a propitiation by His blood, through faith, to demonstrate His righteousness, because in His forbearance God had passed over the sins that were previously committed, to demonstrate at the present time His righteousness, that He might be just and the justifier of the one who has faith in Jesus. (Romans 3:25–26)

Day 4

1. Read Romans 5:1–5. What results of justification does Paul discuss in verses 1–2?

_____

_____

_____

_____

_____

Having been justified by faith, we have peace with God through our Lord Jesus Christ, through whom also we have access by faith into this grace in which we stand, and rejoice in hope of the glory of God. (Romans 5:1–2)

2. What is "hope of the glory of God" (verse 2)? What are we eagerly looking forward to?

_____

_____

_____

_____

_____

Not only that, but we also glory in tribulations, knowing that tribulation produces perseverance; and perseverance, character; and character, hope. Now hope does not disappoint, because the love of God has been poured out in our hearts by the Holy Spirit who was given to us. (Romans 5:3–5)

3. Why does confidence in our justification enable us to glory even in our tribulations (see verse 3)?

_____

_____

_____

_____

_____

_____

4. Have you experienced the process Paul describes in verses 3–5? If so, how are you different as a result? If not, what do you think is missing for you?

_____

_____

_____

_____

_____

_____

_____

God has **implanted** within our hearts evidence that we **belong** to Him in that we love the One who first **loved** us. (*MacArthur Bible Commentary*, page 1520)

5. How can you hang onto and remember the love of God poured out in your heart today? How can you take this amazing gift with you throughout the day?

_____

_____

_____

_____

_____

_____

Day 5

If anyone else thinks he may have confidence in the flesh, I more so. (Philippians 3:4)

1. Read Philippians 3:4–11. What reasons did Paul have for having confidence in who he was by birth, his upbringing, and his behavior (see verses 4–6)?

_____

_____

_____

_____

_____

2. What reasons do you have for being confident in who you are by birth, by upbringing, and by behavior?

_____

_____

_____

_____

_____

3. Why does Paul say he counts those things as loss and rubbish (see verses 7–9)?

_____

_____

_____

_____

_____

But what things were gain to me, these I have counted loss for Christ. Yet indeed I also count all things loss for the excellence of the knowledge of Christ Jesus my Lord, for whom I have suffered the loss of all things, and count them as rubbish. (Philippians 3:7–8)

4. How easy is it for you to count your achievements as rubbish? Why?

_____

_____

_____

_____

_____

5. What does Paul long to know and experience (see verses 10–11)? Why?

_____

_____

_____

_____

_____

_____

I may know Him and the power of His resurrection, and the fellowship of His sufferings, being conformed to His death, if, by any means, I may attain to the resurrection from the dead. (Philippians 3:10–11)

Prayer for the Week

Lord Jesus, You save me not because of any righteous things I've done but solely because of Your mercy. I place no confidence in who I am in the flesh or in anything I've achieved. My confidence is wholly in who You are and what You have achieved by shedding Your blood to atone for my sins. Without that atonement I would be utterly without hope, but with it I have a confident hope of eternal life as Your beloved child. Thank You for making me an heir to everything You possess—the whole universe and the heavenly realm. My faith is in You as my Savior and as the Lord I am committed to obeying. I rush to the Father's throne of grace, asking for the strength to persevere and rejoice in the areas where I suffer. Make me constantly aware of Your love poured out in me through the Holy Spirit. In Your precious name. Amen. ※

A Lesson About
Faithfulness

Watch therefore, for you do not know when the master of the house is coming—in the evening, at midnight, at the crowing of the rooster, or in the morning—lest, coming suddenly, he find you sleeping.

MARK 13:35–36

Main Objectives

In this study, you will (1) identify some of the issues and temptations that come with expectations about the Lord's return, and (2) examine ways to live faithfully in light of the Lord's unknown timetable for His return.

Read and Review

Read chapter 7 from *Parables* and answer the questions that follow. If you're meeting in a small group, you might want to have someone read each of the following excerpts from *Parables* aloud before you discuss the questions related to it.

No One Knows the Hour

The Olivet Discourse is one of the most abused passages anywhere in Scripture. Some interpreters relegate the whole discourse to virtual irrelevance by claiming that all the prophetic words in this section of Scripture were completely fulfilled in AD 70 when Roman armies sacked Jerusalem and destroyed the Jewish temple. (That view is known as preterism.) At the opposite extreme there are those who seem to think today's newspaper is key to understanding the Olivet Discourse. They scour the daily

Mount of Olives: The hill directly opposite the temple. . . .This spot affords the best panoramic view of Jerusalem. (*MacArthur Bible Commentary*, page 1171)

news for "wars and rumors of wars" (Matthew 24:6); "famines, pestilences, and earthquakes in various places" (verse 7); heavenly signs and wonders (verse 29)—or other echoes of this passage. Of course, they never fail to discover fresh reports that seem to fit the passage. Some seem to think the whole discourse is an extended puzzle containing a code that gives a hidden answer to the disciples' question, "When will these things be?" (verse 3). Almost every decade some false prophet comes along who claims to have figured out precisely when the Lord will return.

But Jesus emphatically denies the possibility of such knowledge: "Of that day and hour no one knows, not even the angels of heaven, but My Father only" (verse 36). In fact, Jesus makes this point repeatedly in the Olivet Discourse: "You do not know what hour your Lord is coming" (verse 42). (Parables, page 125)

Take heed, watch and pray; for you do not know when the time is. (Mark 13:33)

1. Why do you think people are so eager to know when the Lord is coming back?

_____

_____

_____

_____

_____

2. Why does the Lord want us *not* to know when He is coming back?

_____

_____

_____

_____

Watch therefore, for you do not know when the master of the house is coming. (Mark 13:35)

3. Have you ever gotten caught up in someone's predictions of when the Lord will return? If so, how did that affect the way you lived? If not, what do you believe keeps you from being drawn into that way of thinking?

_____

_____

_____

_____

_____

The Need for Watchfulness

*The point of the parable [of the wise and foolish virgins] is simple: Christ (the bridegroom) is coming. He may arrive later than we expect, and we must be prepared for that possibility. That means remaining awake, staying at the watch, and being ready for Him no matter how late the hour. In fact, as time passes and His arrival grows closer, the need for watchfulness is greater, not less. The **only** time we can prepare for Him is now, because His sudden arrival will signal the end of all such opportunity. Those not ready for Him when He arrives will be completely and permanently shut out of the wedding feast. (Parables, page 132–133)*

[The foolish virgins'] **absence** was an understandable **annoyance** to the bridegroom. It was inexcusably **thoughtless** of them not to bring oil in the first place. (*Parables*, page 131)

4. According to Ephesians 5:15–20, how are we to prepare for the possibility that Christ may come at any time?

_____

_____

_____

_____

See then that you walk circumspectly, not as fools but as wise, redeeming the time, because the days are evil. (Ephesians 5:15–16)

5. How does Paul exhort his readers in 1 Thessalonians 5:1–10 to prepare for the Lord's coming?

_____

_____

_____

_____

6. If being watchful for the Lord's return doesn't mean scrutinizing the headlines for current events that may herald His coming, what does it mean?

_____

_____

_____

_____

_____

_____

Let us not sleep, as others do, but let us watch and be sober. (1 Thessalonians 5:6)

Settling the Accounts

*[In the parable of the talents,] the time for settling accounts did finally arrive: "After a long time the lord of those servants came" (Matthew 25:19). The faithful servants were commended and rewarded equally. In fact, the master's words to the two faithful servants were identical: "Well done, good and faithful servant; you were faithful over a few things, I will make you ruler over many things. Enter into the joy of your lord" (verses 21, 24). They were honored for their faithfulness—not proportionally based on the size of the profit they earned. That is precisely how Scripture describes the judgment seat of Christ: "Each one will receive his own reward **according to his own labor**"—not according to results (1 Corinthians 3:8, emphasis added).*

The master's response shows him to be a gracious and generous man. He rewarded the faithful stewards with expanded authority, increased opportunity, and a place of joy and favor. Their reward clearly pictures heaven. Heaven is not a place of eternal boredom and tedious inactivity; it is filled with exaltation and honor, expanded opportunities for service, and the greatest joy of all—endless fellowship with Christ Himself. The promises and parables of Jesus are full of similar imagery signifying heaven (cf. Luke 12:35–37, 44; 19:17–19; 22:29–30; John 12:26). (Parables, pages 136–137)

In [Jesus'] culture it was impossible to travel **long distances** on a definite timetable. The servants therefore did not know **precisely** when their master would return, and it seems the trip lasted **longer** than anyone expected. (*Parables*, page 136)

7. Why is it important to know that God will reward us according to our faithful labor, not according to the results we produce?

_____

_____

_____

_____

_____

8. Does it surprise you that heaven is a place of opportunities for service rather than tedious inactivity? What types of service can you imagine doing in heaven?

_____

_____

_____

_____

_____

9. What tends to be your attitude toward work? Do you see it more as a necessary evil or as something that enables you to do things God wants done in the world?

_____

_____

_____

_____

_____

Make the Connection

Read the following Scripture passages and answer the questions provided. If you are meeting in a small group, you might want to have someone read each passage aloud before you discuss the questions related to it.

[Jesus said,] *"Who then is a faithful and wise servant, whom his master made ruler over his household, to give them food in due season? Blessed is that servant whom his master, when he comes, will find so doing. Assuredly, I say to you that he will make him ruler over all his goods.*

"But if that evil servant says in his heart, 'My master is delaying his coming,' and begins to beat his fellow servants, and to eat and drink with the drunkards, the master of that servant will come on a day when he is not looking for him and at an hour that he is not aware of, and will cut him in two and appoint him his portion with the hypocrites. There shall be weeping and gnashing of teeth.

"Then the kingdom of heaven shall be likened to ten virgins who took their lamps and went out to meet the bridegroom. Now five of them were wise, and five were foolish. Those who were foolish took their lamps and

took no oil with them, but the wise took oil in their vessels with their lamps. But while the bridegroom was delayed, they all slumbered and slept.

"And at midnight a cry was heard: 'Behold, the bridegroom is coming; go out to meet him!' Then all those virgins arose and trimmed their lamps. And the foolish said to the wise, 'Give us some of your oil, for our lamps are going out.' But the wise answered, saying, 'No, lest there should not be enough for us and you; but go rather to those who sell, and buy for yourselves.' And while they went to buy, the bridegroom came, and those who were ready went in with him to the wedding; and the door was shut.

"Afterward the other virgins came also, saying, 'Lord, Lord, open to us!'

"But he answered and said, 'Assuredly, I say to you, I do not know you.'

"Watch therefore, for you know neither the day nor the hour in which the Son of Man is coming." (Matthew 24:45—25:13)

The parable of the ten virgins underscores the **importance** of being ready for Christ's **return** in any event, even if He **delays** longer than expected. (*MacArthur Bible Commentary*, page 1174)

10. In the first parable Jesus tells (see 24:45–51), what is the evil servant's error? How does it affect his actions?

_____

_____

_____

_____

_____

11. In the second parable Jesus relates (see 25:1-13), what is the foolish virgins' error? How does it affect their actions?

_____

_____

_____

_____

_____

12. Are you more tempted to live as if the Lord won't return anytime soon, so you can live however you want? Or are you more tempted to live as if He will come soon, so you don't have to plan for the long term? What is the problem with either approach?

Be sober, be vigilant; because your adversary the devil walks about like a roaring lion, seeking whom he may devour. (1 Peter 5:8)

_____

_____

_____

[Jesus said,] "The kingdom of heaven is like a man traveling to a far country, who called his own servants and delivered his goods to them. And to one he gave five talents, to another two, and to another one, to each according to his own ability; and immediately he went on a journey. Then he who had received the five talents went and traded with them, and made another five talents. And likewise he who had received two gained two more also. But he who had received one went and dug in the ground, and hid his lord's

Talent: Not coin or currency but a unit of weight. . . . Even a single talent would be an immense fortune. (*Parables*, page 135)

money. After a long time the lord of those servants came and settled accounts with them.

"So he who had received five talents came and brought five other talents, saying, 'Lord, you delivered to me five talents; look, I have gained five more talents besides them.' His lord said to him, 'Well done, good and faithful servant; you were faithful over a few things, I will make you ruler over many things. Enter into the joy of your lord.' He also who had received two talents came and said, 'Lord, you delivered to me two talents; look, I have gained two more talents besides them.' His lord said to him, 'Well done, good and faithful servant; you have been faithful over a few things, I will make you ruler over many things. Enter into the joy of your lord.'

"Then he who had received the one talent came and said, 'Lord, I knew you to be a hard man, reaping where you have not sown, and gathering where you have not scattered seed. And I was afraid, and went and hid your talent in the ground. Look, there you have what is yours.'

"But his lord answered and said to him, 'You wicked and lazy servant, you knew that I reap where I have not sown, and gather where I have not scattered seed. So you ought to have deposited my money with the bankers, and at my coming I would have received back my own with interest. Therefore take the talent from him, and give it to him who has ten talents.

"'For to everyone who has, more will be given, and he will have abundance; but from him who does not have, even what he has will be taken away. And cast the unprofitable servant into the outer darkness. There will be weeping and gnashing of teeth'" (Matthew 25:14–30).

In contrast to those inclined to **drop out** of life and wait on a hilltop, the faithful believer must continue to **work** and **plan** with an eye to the future. Careful, prudent planning is not antithetical to living by faith. (*Parables*, page 133)

Those who **despise** the riches of God's goodness . . . will ultimately **lose** everything they have. (*MacArthur Bible Commentary*, page 1175)

13. A *talent* was a weight of silver (or other precious metal). Even one talent of silver was a large fortune. What do the talents in this parable represent?

_____

_____

_____

_____

14. What was the unprofitable servant's problem?

_____

_____

_____

_____

Having then gifts differing according to the grace that is given to us, let us use them. (Romans 12:6)

15. What point are we meant to take away from this parable?

_____

_____

_____

_____

Explore the Key Points

Take some time to consider how some of the big ideas of this chapter intersect with your own life. It will be helpful to answer these questions on your own before you discuss them with your group. If you're meeting with a group, you may want to have someone read aloud the key point before you discuss it.

Pictures of Faithfulness

We get three pictures of faithfulness in these three parables. In Matthew 24:45–51, the faithful and wise servant was doing his job feeding the other servants and generally caring for their needs. Part of our job as God's servants is to care for our fellow believers and do whatever work in the world our Master has given us to do. The wise servant is *watchful*, not complacently doubting whether he will ever be held accountable for his actions.

In Matthew 25:1–13, the wise virgins show their faithfulness by planning ahead for the possibility the bridegroom will not come for some extended period of time. We don't ask what the oil represents, because the parable is not an allegory in which each detail symbolizes something. Instead, we ask more broadly, "What does planning ahead look like for us?" If the Lord might not come for another thousand years, what are the implications for the way we lead our lives, the way we use our money, and the way we care for the planet? The wise virgins show the virtue of *waiting*, no matter how long the Lord postpones His coming.

Finally, in Matthew 25:14–30, the first two servants who received the talents traded with them to double their investments. They show the virtue of *working* with whatever God has entrusted to us while we wait for Him. We can ask ourselves, "What has God entrusted to me? How can I invest it in things that matter to Him and contribute to His kingdom agenda?"

> **Faithfulness:** Showing true and constant support or loyalty; deserving trust; keeping your promises or doing what you are supposed to do. (*Merriam-Webster*)

16. Any day now, you may have to face the Lord and give an account for the way you have lived. That day might come because He returns or because you die suddenly. How does knowing this affect the way you live?

> *So then each of us shall give account of himself to God.* (Romans 14:12)

_____

_____

_____

_____

_____

17. What does planning ahead involve for you? How should you live in case the Lord doesn't intend to come for another thousand years?

_____

_____

_____

_____

We are His workmanship, created in Christ Jesus for good works. (Ephesians 2:10)

18. What abilities and assets has God entrusted to you? How can you use them to contribute to His kingdom agenda?

_____

_____

_____

_____

_____

Authentic Believers

All three stories contrast the defining characteristics that set authentic Christians apart from unbelievers: faithfulness versus unbelief; wisdom versus folly; and preparedness versus indifference.

I know your works, that you are neither cold nor hot. I could wish you were cold or hot. (Revelation 3:15)

None of the characters in these parables picture a halfhearted or lukewarm "carnal Christian." That's because Jesus Himself ruled out the possibility that such people exist. In His own words, "He who is not with Me is against Me, and he who does not gather with Me scatters abroad" (Matthew 12:30). A person is not a true believer if he or she has no real expectation of Christ's return, no eagerness to meet Him, and no love for His appearing. In fact, the lessons of these parables are the same lessons that saving grace teaches every true believer: "That, denying ungodliness and worldly lusts, we should live soberly, righteously, and godly in the present age, looking for the blessed hope and glorious appearing of our great God and Savior Jesus Christ" (Titus 2:12–13).

Behold, I am coming quickly, and My reward is with Me, to give to every one according to his work. (Revelation 22:12)

So, the three parables combined give us one clear and powerful message: "You do not know when the master of the house is coming—in the evening, at midnight, at the crowing of the rooster, or in the morning" (Mark 13:35). For this reason, "you also be ready, for the Son of Man is coming at an hour you do not expect" (Matthew 24:44). Meanwhile, keep watching, waiting, and working faithfully.

19. How have you seen other believers being faithful to Christ? What does faithfulness look like in them?

_____

_____

_____

_____

20. How have you tried to be faithful to the Lord? What have you done to show the Lord your faithfulness to Him?

_____

_____

_____

_____

21. What opportunities do you have to be faithful in your relationship with God? With others? With yourself?

_____

_____

_____

_____

_____

_____

But as for you, brethren,
do not grow weary in doing good.
(2 Thessalonians 3:13)

Living the Parable

We've covered a lot in this lesson. Now it is your chance to pull it all together and decide what is the most important principle(s) you need to take to heart. You probably can't change your life in half a dozen ways this week, so prayerfully consider what is God's top priority for you.

22. What is your main takeaway(s) from this lesson? What do you want to take to heart as you go forward?

_____

_____

_____

_____

_____

_____

_____

23. What are some things you will do to apply what you've learned?

_____

_____

_____

_____

_____

_____

Reflect and Respond

At the end of each lesson, you will find suggested Scripture readings for spending time alone with God during five days of the coming week. Each day of this week's readings will deal with the theme of living faithful lives while we eagerly await Christ's return. Read each passage slowly, pausing to think about what is being said. Rather than approaching this as an assignment to complete, think of it as an encounter with your heavenly Father. Use any of the questions that are helpful.

Whether Christ returns **early** or **late**, He should find us **busy** for Him. (*Parables*, page 135)

Day 1

Owe no one anything except to love one another, for he who loves another has fulfilled the law.
(Romans 13:8)

1. Read Romans 13:8–14. When Paul says love is the fulfillment of the law, is he saying it's unimportant for those who are saved by grace through faith? Why or why not?

_____

_____

_____

_____

_____

_____

Do this, knowing the time, that now it is high time to awake out of sleep.
(Romans 13:11)

2. How does Paul express the urgency of doing what he says?

_____

_____

_____

_____

_____

Let us walk properly, as in the day, not in revelry and drunkenness, not in lewdness and lust, not in strife and envy. (Romans 13:13)

3. What is strife? Why is it a work of darkness worth singling out for rejection?

_____

_____

_____

_____

_____

4. What is envy? Why is it a work of darkness worth singling out for rejection?

_____

_____

_____

_____

_____

Put on the Lord Jesus Christ, and make no provision for the flesh.
(Romans 13:14)

5. How can you put into practice the faithful living that Paul describes?

_____

_____

_____

_____

Day 2

1. Read Ephesians 4:1–6. What is the calling with which we were called (see verse 1)?

_____

_____

_____

_____

I . . . beseech you to walk worthy of the calling with which you were called, with all lowliness and gentleness, with longsuffering, bearing with one another in love, endeavoring to keep the unity of the Spirit in the bond of peace. (Ephesians 4:1–2)

2. What qualities does Paul list that are worthy of our calling?

_____

_____

_____

_____

_____

3. Why are lowliness and gentleness so important for a faithful way of life?

_____

_____

_____

_____

_____

4. Paul emphasizes "the unity of the Spirit" (verse 4). Why is this so important in a Christian community?

_____

_____

_____

_____

_____

There is one body and one Spirit, just as you were called in one hope of your calling. (Ephesians 4:4)

5. How can you put into practice the faithful living that Paul describes?

_____

_____

_____

_____

_____

Day 3

1. Read Ephesians 4:17–24. What is wrong with the way unbelievers perceive and think about the world (see verses 17–19)?

_____

_____

_____

_____

No longer walk as the rest of the Gentiles walk, in the futility of their mind, having their understanding darkened. (Ephesians 4:17–18)

But you have not so learned Christ, if indeed you have heard Him and have been taught by Him. (Ephesians 4:20–21)

2. How is the way Christians think about the world different?

_____

_____

_____

3. What does it mean to be "renewed in the spirit of your mind" (verse 23)?

_____

_____

_____

_____

Put on the new man which was created according to God, in true righteousness and holiness. (Ephesians 4:24)

4. How is that renewal essential for faithful living?

_____

_____

_____

5. How can you demonstrate the renewal of the spirit of your mind today?

_____

_____

_____

_____

_____

Day 4

"Let each one of you speak truth." . . . "Be angry, and do not sin." . . . Let him who stole steal no longer. . . . Let no corrupt word proceed out of your mouth. (Ephesians 4:25–26, 28–29)

1. Read Ephesians 4:25–32. As you read this description of faithful living, what aspects come easily to you as habits you have already formed?

_____

_____

_____

_____

2. Are there any parts of this description that you are still growing in? If so, what are they?

_____

_____

_____

_____

3. How does a person grieve the Holy Spirit (see verse 30)?

_____

_____

_____

_____

Do not grieve the Holy Spirit of God, by whom you were sealed for the day of redemption. (Ephesians 4:30)

4. Why do you think our speech is such an important area of faithful living? Why do you think Paul calls attention to it in this passage more than once (see verses 25, 29)?

_____

_____

_____

_____

_____

_____

Let all bitterness, wrath, anger, clamor, and evil speaking be put away from you, with all malice. And be kind to one another, tenderhearted, forgiving one another, even as God in Christ forgave you. (Ephesians 4:31–32)

5. What is one way you can put Paul's instructions into practice today?

_____

_____

_____

_____

Day 5

1. Read Colossians 3:12–17. Why is it important that these instructions are for "the elect of God, holy and beloved" (verse 12)?

_____

_____

_____

_____

_____

As the elect of God . . . put on tender mercies, kindness, humility, meekness, longsuffering. (Colossians 3:12)

2. Why is bearing with one another so crucial?

_____

_____

_____

Bearing with one another, and forgiving one another. (Colossians 3:13)

3. What does it mean to "let the peace of God rule in your heart" (verse 15)?

_____

_____

_____

Let the peace of God rule in your hearts . . . and be thankful. (Colossians 3:15)

Let the word of Christ dwell in you . . . teaching and admonishing one another in psalms and hymns and spiritual songs, singing with grace in your hearts to the Lord.
(Colossians 3:16)

4. What value does Paul place on psalms and worship music (see verse 16)? Why do you think he values them?

_____

_____

_____

_____

_____

Whatever you do in word or deed, do all in the name of the Lord Jesus, giving thanks to God the Father through Him.
(Colossians 3:17)

5. Paul mentions thankfulness twice (see verses 15, 17). How can a person make thankfulness a habit?

_____

_____

_____

_____

Prayer for the Week

Dear Lord, help me to be faithful to You in all my thoughts, words, and actions. I want to put on the armor of light and walk properly, as in the day. I want to eagerly anticipate Your coming and be fully prepared no matter how soon You come. Show me how to walk worthy of my calling. Form in me the habits of a fully renewed mind. Help me embrace the opportunities to bear with others, to forgive them, and to be kind to them. Thank You for granting me salvation when I was deluded in my thinking. Thank You for taking off the blinders from my eyes. Let my life overflow with gratitude for Your saving grace. In our Lord Jesus' name. Amen. ✳

A Lesson About
Serpentine Wisdom

So the master commended the unjust steward because
he had dealt shrewdly. For the sons of this world are more shrewd
in their generation than the sons of light.

LUKE 16:8

Main Objectives

In this study, you will (1) look at how to use worldly wealth to "gain friends" in eternity, and (2) examine what *shrewdness* is and how it can be a positive trait if directed in the right way.

Read and Review

Read chapter 8 from *Parables* and answer the questions that follow. If you're meeting in a small group, you might want to have someone read each of the following excerpts from *Parables* aloud before you discuss the questions related to it.

The Love of Money

Scripture emphatically condemns the love of money. "For the love of money is a root of all kinds of evil, for which some have strayed from the faith in their greediness, and pierced themselves through with many sorrows. But you, O man of God, flee these things and pursue righteousness, godliness, faith, love, patience, gentleness" (1 Timothy 6:10–11).

Roughly a **third** of the forty or so parables Jesus told have something to do with **earthly riches**. (*Parables*, page 141)

Jesus commends the use of **financial** assets for **heavenly** and eternal purposes. (*MacArthur Bible Commentary*, page 1133)

Jesus summed up His teaching on the matter in one clear exhortation in His Sermon on the Mount: "Do not lay up for yourselves treasures on earth, where moth and rust destroy and where thieves break in and steal; but lay up for yourselves treasures in heaven, where neither moth nor rust destroys and where thieves do not break in and steal. For where your treasure is, there your heart will be also" (Matthew 6:19–21). (Parables, page 142)

1. How does the love of money conflict with righteousness, godliness, faith, love, generosity, and gentleness?

_____

_____

_____

_____

_____

2. What are the risks of laying up treasures for ourselves on earth?

_____

_____

_____

_____

Keep your lives free from the love of money and be content with what you have. (Hebrews 13:5 NIV)

3. Does saving money for investments such as retirement or college conflict with Jesus' teaching not to lay up treasures for ourselves on earth? Why or why not?

_____

_____

_____

_____

_____

_____

Shrewd Resourcefulness

Then Jesus plainly states His whole point. "The sons of this world are more shrewd in their generation than the sons of light" (Luke 16:8). Sinners tend to be more clever and forward thinking and diligent with regard to their short-term temporal well-being than saints are in the work of laying up treasure for eternity. That's the whole point as stated succinctly by Jesus Himself. "Sons of this world" are those who have no part and no interest in the kingdom of God. They have nothing to look forward to except the remaining years of their earthly lives. But they are more concerned and more clever when it comes to securing an advantageous future for their retirement years than the "sons of light," who have an eternal future to prepare for. It's true. Ungodly people bring amazing energy, skill, and focus to the task of acquiring earthly comforts for the remaining years of this life. Mainly because that's all they really have to look forward to.

In Luke 16, [*Mammon*] is used for "**riches**." Mammon is also considered an **idol** or **god** of the human heart that is in conflict with the true God. The Bible proclaims it is **impossible** to serve this god of the world and the **true God** at the same time. (*MacArthur Bible Commentary*, page 1311)

The expression "sons of light" is a common New Testament phrase that designates true disciples of Christ—redeemed people (John 12:36; Ephesians 5:8; 1 Thessalonians 5:5). After all, "our citizenship is in heaven, from which we also eagerly wait for the Savior, the Lord Jesus Christ" (Philippians 3:20). It is therefore right that we should have our minds "set . . . on things above, not on things on the earth" (Colossians 3:2). Yet compared to all the strategizing, maneuvering, twisting, and turning unbelievers go through to secure their future in this world, "the sons of light" display a distinct lack of wisdom.

Consider how absurd that is. People preparing for retirement probably have (at most) three decades to plan for—usually much less. Life is short and "the world is passing away, and the lust of it" (1 John 2:17). Yet "the sons of this world" will go to almost any length to gain whatever advantage they can for the waning years of their lives. Their worldliness and their lack of scruples are not what Jesus commends. Their shrewd resourcefulness is. Surely "sons of light," bound for eternity, ought to be more active, more zealous, more mindful, and more wise about redeeming the time, preparing for the future, and laying up treasure in heaven. (*Parables*, pages 150–151)

Become sons of light. (John 12:36)

Walk as children of light. (Ephesians 5:8)

You are all sons of light. (1 Thessalonians 5:5)

Resourceful: Able to deal well with new or difficult situations and to find solutions to problems. (*Merriam-Webster*)

4. Why are the "sons of this world" so careful and foresighted about planning for their earthly futures?

_____
_____
_____
_____
_____

5. Why do you think the "sons of light" aren't often as equally foresighted about investing in their eternal futures?

_____
_____
_____
_____
_____

6. What does it mean to lay up treasure in heaven?

_____
_____
_____
_____
_____

He who loves silver will not be satisfied with silver; nor he who loves abundance, with increase. (Ecclesiastes 5:10)

A Resource for the Good of Others

Immediately after commending the shrewdness of the sons of this world for their forward-thinking resourcefulness, Jesus adds this word of advice for His disciples: "And I say to you, make friends for yourselves by unrighteous mammon, that when

Believers are to use their Master's **money** in a way that will accrue friends for **eternity**—by investing in the kingdom gospel that brings sinners to **salvation**. (*MacArthur Bible Commentary*, page 1312)

[it fails], they may receive you into an everlasting home" (Luke 16:9). Use your money to make friends—not earthly friends, but friends who will welcome you into your eternal home. In other words, be generous with the people of God. Put your money to work for others; help the truly needy among God's people; "and you will have treasure in heaven" (Matthew 19:21). Remember the words of Jesus in Matthew 25:35–40: "I was hungry and you gave Me food; I was thirsty and you gave Me drink; I was a stranger and you took Me in; I was naked and you clothed Me; I was sick and you visited Me; I was in prison and you came to Me. . . . Inasmuch as you did it to one of the least of **these My brethren**, you did it to Me" (emphasis added).

This also underscores our duty to use our money to support the ministry of the gospel. Will people be standing on the edge of glory when you arrive, eager to embrace you, because through your investment in gospel ministry and the extension of the kingdom they heard and believed and gained eternal life in Christ? That's the imagery Jesus' exhortation evokes. (*Parables*, pages 151–152)

All who believed were together, and had all things in common, and sold their possessions and goods, and divided them among all, as anyone had need. (Acts 2:44–45)

7. How can we use worldly wealth to gain friends for ourselves in our eternal home?

_____
_____
_____
_____
_____
_____

8. What shift in our thinking is required in order for us to treat money as a resource to be used for the good of others?

_____
_____
_____
_____
_____
_____

Since we are surrounded by so great a cloud of witnesses, let us lay aside every weight. (Hebrews 12:1)

9. Take a moment to imagine going to heaven and being embraced by people who heard and believed in Christ because of your investment in gospel ministry. What thoughts, images, and feelings does that evoke in you?

_____
_____
_____
_____
_____
_____
_____

Make the Connection

Read the following Scripture passages and answer the questions provided. If you are meeting in a small group, you might want to have someone read each passage aloud before you discuss the questions related to it.

[Jesus] also said to His disciples: "There was a certain rich man who had a steward, and an accusation was brought to him that this man was wasting his goods. So he called him and said to him, 'What is this I hear about you? Give an account of your stewardship, for you can no longer be steward.'

"Then the steward said within himself, 'What shall I do? For my master is taking the stewardship away from me. I cannot dig; I am ashamed to beg. I have resolved what to do, that when I am put out of the stewardship, they may receive me into their houses.'

"So he called every one of his master's debtors to him, and said to the first, 'How much do you owe my master?' And he said, 'A hundred measures of oil.' So he said to him, 'Take your bill, and sit down quickly and write fifty.' Then he said to another, 'And how much do you owe?' So he said, 'A hundred measures of wheat.' And he said to him, 'Take your bill, and write eighty.' So the master commended the unjust steward because he had dealt shrewdly. For the sons of this world are more shrewd in their generation than the sons of light." (Luke 16:1–8)

> **Steward:** A steward was a trusted servant, usually someone born in the household, who was chief of the management and distribution of household provisions. (*MacArthur Bible Commentary*, page 1311)

10. How was the steward shrewd? What did he do that demonstrated shrewdness?

_____

_____

_____

_____

_____

_____

> The sheer **cleverness** of the scheme was what elicited the master's **admiration**. The steward took careful **advantage** of a brief and fleeting opportunity. (*Parables*, page 149)

11. What is shocking about this parable?

_____

_____

_____

_____

_____

12. Why do you suppose Jesus deliberately shocked His disciples in this way?

_____

_____

_____

_____

_____

> *The disciples were astonished at His words. (Mark 10:24)*

Many of the **Pharisees** taught that devotion to **money** and devotion to God were perfectly **compatible**. (*MacArthur Bible Commentary*, page 1312)

[Jesus said,] "I tell you, use worldly wealth to gain friends for yourselves, so that when it is gone, you will be welcomed into eternal dwellings.

"Whoever can be trusted with very little can also be trusted with much, and whoever is dishonest with very little will also be dishonest with much. So if you have not been trustworthy in handling worldly wealth, who will trust you with true riches? And if you have not been trustworthy with someone else's property, who will give you property of your own?

"No one can serve two masters. Either you will hate the one and love the other, or you will be devoted to the one and despise the other. You cannot serve both God and money." (Luke 16:9–13 NIV)

13. How can we demonstrate to God that we can be trusted with the money He has given us?

_____

_____

_____

_____

_____

_____

It is required in stewards that one be found faithful. (1 Corinthians 4:2)

14. Why does Jesus speak about "someone else's property" (verse 12)? In what sense have we been entrusted with someone else's property?

_____

_____

_____

_____

_____

_____

Serve: To give the service and respect due to (a superior); to comply with the commands or demands of. (*Merriam-Webster*)

15. What does it mean to "serve" money (verse 13)?

_____

_____

_____

_____

_____

Explore the Key Points

Take some time to consider how some of the big ideas of this chapter intersect with your own life. It will be helpful to answer these questions on your own before you discuss them with your group. If you're meeting with a group, you may want to have someone read aloud the key point before you discuss it.

The Value of Shrewdness

The master didn't admire the steward's selfishness or wickedness—he admired his shrewdness. Shrewdness is cleverness, canniness, prudence, knowing how the world works, and living accordingly. The Greek word, *phronimos*, has the idea of being cautious, keen-witted, and circumspect. The steward's plan was wickedly ingenious. The steward took careful advantage of a brief and fleeting opportunity. He manipulated what resources were temporarily in his power to achieve ends that were to his long-term advantage. He used the master's resources to do those debtors immense good. He won their friendship with lavish generosity.

Jesus wants His disciples to have that same kind of forward-looking ingenuity, but focused on eternal realities. He wants us to know how the world works (with eternal rewards and punishments) and to live accordingly. He wants us to take careful advantage of this brief life to secure our eternal future. He wants us to use the material resources we have to achieve eternal ends by investing them in kingdom ventures, for those investments are what will prove to be to our long-term advantage. Jesus wants us to think beyond our senior years in this life and plan carefully and shrewdly for the next life. He wants us to use God's resources (and everything we have is God's) to do immense good for others.

*Christ did not commend the man's **dishonesty**. . . . He only used him as an illustration to show that even the **most wicked** sons of this world are shrewd enough to **provide** for themselves against coming **evil**. (MacArthur Bible Commentary, page 1312)*

Trust in the LORD, and do good; dwell in the land, and feed on His faithfulness. (Psalm 37:3)

16. How is shrewdness in itself a virtue that can be put to good or evil ends?

_____

_____

_____

_____

_____

17. What is an example of a practice that would be considered shrewd if there were no God and eternal life, but not shrewd if there is a God and an eternal destiny?

_____

_____

_____

_____

_____

18. What is an example of the reverse—a practice that is shrewd if God and eternal destiny are real but not shrewd if they aren't?

*Endless personal accumulation is **sinful** and **wasteful**, and it robs us of eternal blessing. (Parables, page 153)*

_____

_____

_____

_____

The Importance of Stewardship

Everything we possess ultimately belongs to God. He has entrusted it to us to use wisely by His standards. "'The silver is Mine, and the gold is Mine,' says the LORD of hosts" (Haggai 2:8). "The earth is the LORD's, and all its fullness, the world and those who dwell therein" (Psalm 24:1). The psalmist says to God, "The earth is full of Your possessions" (Psalm 104:24). God has entrusted us with much or little to be invested in the good of others and the glory of God.

Also, everything we have is temporary. "We brought nothing into this world, and it is certain we can carry nothing out" (1 Timothy 6:7). Those who are not investing in the work of redemption are shirking their duty to be faithful stewards, wasting this passing moment of opportunity, and impoverishing themselves in eternity. God doesn't reward people for frittering away His resources. To spend money on creature comforts and worthless diversions is to rob ourselves of true and eternal riches.

The tragic irony of self-indulgence is that the more we waste on ourselves in the here and now, the less treasure we will have in heaven. The true riches are over there. "We do not look at the things which are seen, but at the things which are not seen. For the things which are seen are temporary, but the things which are not seen are eternal" (2 Corinthians 4:18).

Whether we have much or little, we will have to give an account for what we do with it. True character is seen in how we handle the small things. "He who is faithful in what is least is faithful also in much; and he who is unjust in what is least is unjust also in much" (Luke 16:10). Truly faithful people are generous because of their character, not their circumstances. If we see the immense value of investing in eternity, we will do it with whatever resources we have—in small ways if our resources are small, and in bigger ways if our resources are greater.

> The things we call our own are ultimately **God's** possessions, not ours. . . . They are **divine blessings** held in trust, to be invested as wisely as possible for the good of **others** and the **glory** of God. (*Parables*, page 154)

> **Generosity**, by God's blessing, secures **increase**, while **stinginess** leads to **poverty** instead of expected gain. (*MacArthur Bible Commentary*, page 709)

19. What are the implications of the fact that everything you possess belongs to God and He has entrusted it to you? What difference does that make in the way you spend?

_____

_____

_____

_____

_____

_____

> *Riches do not profit in the day of wrath, but righteousness delivers from death.* (Proverbs 11:4)

20. What makes it harder for you to live as if true riches are the riches of eternity? What makes it easier?

_____

_____

_____

_____

_____

21. What is the immense value of investing in eternity?

_____

_____

_____

_____

_____

Heaven and earth will pass away, but My words will by no means pass away. (Matthew 24:35)

Living the Parable

We've covered a lot in this lesson. Now it is your chance to pull it all together and decide what is the most important principle(s) you need to take to heart. You probably can't change your life in half a dozen ways this week, so prayerfully consider what is God's top priority for you.

22. What is your main takeaway(s) from this lesson? What do you want to take to heart as you go forward?

_____

_____

_____

_____

23. What are some things you will do to apply what you've learned?

_____

_____

_____

_____

Reflect and Respond

At the end of each lesson, you will find suggested Scripture readings for spending time alone with God during five days of the coming week. Each day of this week's readings will deal with the theme of money. Read each passage slowly, pausing to think about what is being said. Rather than approaching this as an assignment to complete, think of it as an encounter with your heavenly Father. Use any of the questions that are helpful.

Jesus refers to money as "the **unrighteous** mammon" because earthly riches belong to this fallen, **transient** world. (*Parables*, page 152)

Day 1

1. Read 1 Timothy 6:6–10. What is *contentment*?

_____

_____

_____

Godliness with contentment is great gain. For we brought nothing into this world, and it is certain we can carry nothing out.
(1 Timothy 1:6–7)

Having food and clothing, with these we shall be content.
(1 Timothy 1:8)

Those who desire to be rich fall into temptation and a snare, and into many foolish and harmful lusts. . . . The love of money is a root of all kinds of evil, for which some have strayed from the faith in their greediness, and pierced themselves through with many sorrows.
(1 Timothy 6:9–10)

One from the crowd said to Him, "Teacher, tell my brother to divide the inheritance with me." . . . He spoke a parable to them, saying: "The ground of a certain rich man yielded plentifully."
(Luke 12:13, 16)

2. Why does Paul say "godliness with contentment is great gain" (verse 6)?

_____

_____

_____

_____

_____

3. Can you imagine being content with just food and clothing? Why or why not?

_____

_____

_____

_____

_____

4. Why is the desire to be rich such a snare to us?

_____

_____

_____

_____

5. What are some examples of the evils that grow from the love of money?

_____

_____

_____

_____

_____

_____

Day 2

1. Read Luke 12:13–21. What were the circumstances that led Jesus to tell this parable?

_____

_____

_____

_____

2. Why was the rich man in this parable a fool?

_____

_____

_____

_____

3. What does Jesus say through this parable to the man who wanted his brother to divide the inheritance with him?

_____

_____

_____

_____

_____

[The rich man] said, "I will do this: I will pull down my barns and build greater. . . . And I will say to my soul, 'Soul, you have many goods laid up for many years; take your ease; eat, drink, and be merry.'" But God said to him, "Fool! This night your soul will be required of you; then whose will those things be which you have provided?" (Luke 12:17–20)

4. What does Jesus say through the parable to the brother who was resisting dividing the inheritance?

_____

_____

_____

_____

_____

_____

5. How do we go about being rich toward God?

_____

_____

_____

_____

_____

So is he who lays up treasure for himself, and is not rich toward God. (Luke 17:21)

Day 3

1. Read Luke 12:22–31. What reasons for not worrying about bodily needs does Jesus give in this passage?

_____

_____

_____

_____

_____

Consider the ravens, for they neither sow nor reap, which have neither storehouse nor barn; and God feeds them. Of how much more value are you than the birds? . . . Consider the lilies, how they grow: they neither toil nor spin; and yet I say to you, even Solomon in all his glory was not arrayed like one of these. (Luke 12:24, 27)

2. How convincing do you find His reasons? Does your heart easily say yes to His counsel, or does it say yes but with some conditions? If so, what are the conditions?

_____

_____

_____

_____

_____

3. How does Jesus reply to your "conditions" in this passage?

_____
_____
_____
_____
_____

Do not seek what you should eat or what you should drink, nor have an anxious mind. For all these things the nations of the world seek after, and your Father knows that you need these things. But seek the kingdom of God, and all these things shall be added to you.
(Luke 12:29–31)

4. What does it mean to "seek the kingdom of God" (verse 31)?

_____
_____
_____
_____

5. What opportunities do you have to seek the kingdom of God today?

_____
_____
_____
_____
_____
_____

Day 4

Sell what you have and give alms; provide yourselves money bags which do not grow old, a treasure in the heavens that does not fail, where no thief approaches nor moth destroys. (Luke 12:33)

1. Read Luke 12:32–34. How do you respond to Jesus' instruction to "sell what you have and give alms" (verse 33)?

_____
_____
_____
_____
_____
_____

2. What reasons does Jesus provide for giving your money to the needy?

_____
_____
_____
_____

For where your treasure is, there your heart will be also.
(Luke 12:34)

3. Where is your treasure? Where is your heart?

_____
_____
_____
_____

4. Do you think Jesus wants all Christians to sell all their possessions and give the proceeds to the needy? Explain.

_____

_____

_____

_____

_____

_____

_____

5. What place does giving to the needy have in your spending habits?

_____

_____

_____

_____

_____

He who has pity on the poor lends to the Lord, and He will pay back what he has given. (Proverbs 19:17)

Day 5

1. Read 2 Corinthians 9:6–11. What does Paul mean when he states, "He who sows sparingly will also reap sparingly, and he who sows bountifully will also reap bountifully" (verse 6)?

_____

_____

_____

_____

_____

_____

2. Why is it important to give cheerfully, not grudgingly?

_____

_____

_____

_____

_____

So let each one give as he purposes in his heart, not grudgingly or of necessity; for God loves a cheerful giver. (2 Corinthians 9:7)

3. Do you believe God will make sure you have enough to live on? What helps you believe that? What gets in the way?

_____

_____

_____

_____

God is able to make all grace abound toward you, that you, always having all sufficiency in all things. (2 Corinthians 9:8)

May He who supplies seed to the sower, and bread for food, supply and multiply the seed you have sown and increase the fruits of your righteousness, while you are enriched in everything for all liberality, which causes thanksgiving through us to God.
(2 Corinthians 9:10–11)

4. Have you ever experienced God increasing the fruits of your righteousness (see verse 10)? If so, what did this look like?

_____

_____

_____

_____

_____

5. What are the main things you have gained from studying money this week?

_____

_____

_____

_____

Prayer for the Week

Dear Lord, help me to be content with the material things I have and not yearn for more. Protect me from the love of money. Shield me from covetousness and the belief that my life is defined by my possessions. Show me how to be rich toward You. Guard me from worrying about whether I'll have enough. I want to seek Your kingdom—please show me how. If You want me to sell or give away some of my possessions, or if You want me to be more generous with those in need, guide me as to who and how much. I want to be a cheerful giver and enthusiastically generous. Help me to treasure what You treasure. In our Lord Jesus' name. Amen. ✳

A Lesson About
Heaven and Hell

*If they do not hear Moses and the prophets, neither will they
be persuaded though one rise from the dead.*

LUKE 16:31

Main Objectives

In this study, you will (1) explore what Jesus says about hell so you can be diligent in encouraging others to repent and experience eternal life with God, and (2) reflect on the sufficiency of Scripture as you reach out to unbelievers and share the gospel.

Read and Review

Read chapter 9 from *Parables* and answer the questions that follow. If you're meeting in a small group, you might want to have someone read each of the following excerpts from *Parables* aloud before you discuss the questions related to it.

The Reality of Hell

No one in the Bible had more to say about hell than the Savior of sinners, the Lord Jesus Christ. The most vivid and detailed biblical descriptions of hell appear in the four Gospels, and they come from Jesus. Other New Testament authors allude to the reality of hell, but the substance of what we know about it comes mainly from Jesus' public discourses (with occasional references drawn from the private instruction He

[Jesus] indicated that *most* of this world's **religious** activity is nothing more than a **highway to hell.** (*Parables*, page 158)

The Pharisees were perhaps the most **biblically** oriented religious leaders of their time, and yet they **epitomized** what Jesus was warning about. (*Parables*, page 158)

gave to the Twelve). Our Lord had much more to say about hell than the average person might think—and a lot of what He taught about hell is profoundly shocking.

He indicated, for example, that hell will be full of religious people. According to Scripture, multitudes of seemingly devout and philanthropic people (including some self-styled miracle workers) will be astonished when they are turned away at the throne of judgment.

Jesus made that point emphatically: "Not everyone who says to Me, 'Lord, Lord,' shall enter the kingdom of heaven, but he who does the will of My Father in heaven. Many will say to Me in that day, 'Lord, Lord, have we not prophesied in Your name, cast out demons in Your name, and done many wonders in Your name?' And then I will declare to them, 'I never knew you; depart from Me, you who practice lawlessness!'" (Matthew 7:21–23). Those turned away will include not only people who are ensnared in cults and false religions, but also confessionally orthodox people who don't truly believe what they profess. Such people cover their unbelief and secret sins with a veneer of hypocritical religiosity. (*Parables*, page 158)

The **souls** of the **unsaved** at death are kept under punishment until the final **resurrection**. . . . They shall then appear at the Great White Throne **judgment** and shall be cast into hell, the **lake of fire.** (*MacArthur Bible Commentary*, page xviii)

1. Why do you think some people are surprised that most of what we know about hell comes from Jesus?

_____

_____

_____

_____

_____

_____

2. What does it say about Jesus that He would talk so much and so graphically about hell?

_____

_____

_____

_____

_____

_____

_____

As the body without the spirit is dead, so faith without works is dead also. (James 2:26)

3. Jesus says, "Not everyone who says to Me, 'Lord, Lord,' shall enter the kingdom of heaven, but he who does the will of My Father in heaven" (Matthew 7:21). What is the will of the Father that we need to do in order to enter the kingdom of heaven?

_____

_____

_____

_____

_____

_____

The Terror of the Lord

Of course, hell has always stirred negative passions. That was true even in Jesus' time. But today the subject is virtually taboo—even in supposedly evangelical circles. Hell is an embarrassment to those who want Christianity to fit the modern dogmas of universal goodwill and broad-minded tolerance. It is an inconvenience to those who want the biblical message to always sound cheerful to unchurched people. It is an irritant to those who want a religion that makes people always feel good about themselves. And it is an offense to those who care little about righteousness and don't really fear God—but want to maintain some pretense of piety anyway.

Because opinions such as those are so widespread, countless church leaders today think they need to downplay what the Bible says about hell (or totally ignore it). Most of the popular tracts and evangelism programs produced over the past hundred years intentionally sidestep any mention of the horrors of hell. The goal, supposedly, is to give greater emphasis to the love of God—as if to exonerate Him from the reproach of what He Himself says in His own Word. (Parables, page 163)

Dogma: A belief or set of beliefs that is accepted by the members of a group without being questioned. (*Merriam-Webster*)

Fear Him who is able to destroy both soul and body in hell. (Matthew 10:28)

4. What place does hell have in the preaching and teaching at your church? Why do you think that is the case?

_____

_____

_____

_____

_____

_____

_____

_____

5. Why is it important to teach clearly about the horrors of hell?

_____

_____

_____

_____

_____

_____

Anyone not found written in the Book of Life was cast into the lake of fire. (Revelation 20:15)

6. How do you personally respond to teaching about hell? Does it frighten you? Offend you? Draw you closer to Christ? Push you away? Explain.

_____

_____

_____

_____

_____

_____

_____

_____

Everlasting Punishment

*The Word of God **does** say often and categorically that He will punish evildoers with "everlasting punishment" (Matthew 25:46) by "everlasting fire" (verse 41). The Bible describes hell repeatedly as a place "where 'Their worm does not die and the fire is not quenched'" (Mark 9:48, quoting Isaiah 66:24). Revelation 14:10–11 says any person who receives the mark of the Beast during the Great Tribulation "shall be tormented with fire and brimstone in the presence of the holy angels and in the presence of the Lamb. And the smoke of their torment ascends forever and ever; and they have no rest day or night."*

So hell is consistently described as a place of never-ending affliction: "These will go away into everlasting punishment, but the righteous into eternal life" (Matthew 25:46). The word translated "everlasting" is aiōnios. It is exactly the same Greek word translated "eternal" near the end of that same verse. In other words, the "everlasting punishment" of the wicked lasts precisely as long as the "eternal life" of the redeemed. Aiōnios is also the word used of God's glory in 1 Peter 5:10 ("His eternal glory by Christ Jesus"). And it is used of God Himself in Romans 16:26 ("the everlasting God"). The way that word is consistently used in the Bible means it simply cannot be redefined or reinterpreted to accommodate the notion of a finite time span. (Parables, pages 164–165)

> Even a few . . . Christian **leaders** and Bible **commentators** have sometimes complained that the idea of hell seems **cruel** or **unfair**. They wonder how a truly loving God could ever send people into **everlasting punishment**.
> (*Parables*, page 164)

> The punishment of the **wicked** is as **never-ending** as the bliss of the righteous. The wicked are not given a **second chance**, nor are they annihilated.
> (*MacArthur Bible Commentary*, page 1176)

7. Why is it important to understand that hell is a place of everlasting affliction?

_____

_____

_____

_____

> *These shall be punished with everlasting destruction from the presence of the Lord and from the glory of His power.*
> (1 Thessalonians 1:9)

8. Given the teaching of Scripture, why do some people nonetheless prefer to believe that hell is a place of temporary suffering?

_____

_____

_____

_____

_____

9. How does this teaching affect you personally? Will it affect anything you do?

_____

_____

_____

_____

_____

Make the Connection

Read the following Scripture passages and answer the questions provided. If you are meeting in a small group, you might want to have someone read each passage aloud before you discuss the questions related to it.

[Jesus said,] "There was a certain rich man who was clothed in purple and fine linen and fared sumptuously every day. But there was a certain beggar named Lazarus, full of sores, who was laid at his gate, desiring to be fed with the crumbs which fell from the rich man's table. Moreover the dogs came and licked his sores. So it was that the beggar died, and was carried by the angels to Abraham's bosom. The rich man also died and was buried. And being in torments in Hades, he lifted up his eyes and saw Abraham afar off, and Lazarus in his bosom.

"Then he cried and said, 'Father Abraham, have mercy on me, and send Lazarus that he may dip the tip of his finger in water and cool my tongue; for I am tormented in this flame.' But Abraham said, 'Son, remember that in your lifetime you received your good things, and likewise Lazarus evil things; but now he is comforted and you are tormented. And besides all this, between us and you there is a great gulf fixed, so that those who want to pass from here to you cannot, nor can those from there pass to us.'

"Then he said, 'I beg you therefore, father, that you would send him to my father's house, for I have five brothers, that he may testify to them, lest they also come to this place of torment.' Abraham said to him, 'They have Moses and the prophets; let them hear them.' And he said, 'No, father Abraham; but if one goes to them from the dead, they will repent.' But he said to him, 'If they do not hear Moses and the prophets, neither will they be persuaded though one rise from the dead.'" (Luke 16:19–31)

10. What can we learn about hell from this parable?

_____

_____

_____

_____

_____

_____

11. What point is Jesus making in telling this parable?

_____

_____

_____

_____

_____

_____

Lazarus: This beggar was the only character in any of Jesus' parables ever given a name. (*MacArthur Bible Commentary*, page 1313)

Abraham's bosom: Lazarus was given a place of high honor, reclining next to Abraham at the heavenly banquet. (*MacArthur Bible Commentary*, page 1313)

This is indeed a **parable**, not a true story about something that **literally** happened. . . . We know from other clear statements of Scripture that people in hell cannot **see** into heaven and **observe** or **recognize** people there. (*Parables*, page 166)

Since **unbelief** is at heart a spiritual, rather than an intellectual, problem, no amount of **evidences** will ever turn unbelief to **faith.** (*MacArthur Bible Commentary*, page 1314)

12. Why do you suppose the rich man doesn't repent of his sinful attitudes?

_____

_____

_____

_____

_____

_____

Repent, and let every one of you be baptized in the name of Jesus Christ for the remission of sins. (Acts 2:38)

In those last few days before His death, the scene in John's Gospel changes from **hatred** and **rejection** to an unmistakable and blessed witness of the **glory** of Christ. All the rejection and hatred could not dim His glory as displayed through the **resurrection** of Lazarus. (*MacArthur Bible Commentary*, page 1394)

Then Jesus, again groaning in Himself, came to the tomb. It was a cave, and a stone lay against it. Jesus said, "Take away the stone."

Martha, the sister of him who was dead, said to Him, "Lord, by this time there is a stench, for he has been dead four days."

Jesus said to her, "Did I not say to you that if you would believe you would see the glory of God?" Then they took away the stone from the place where the dead man was lying. And Jesus lifted up His eyes and said, "Father, I thank You that You have heard Me. And I know that You always hear Me, but because of the people who are standing by I said this, that they may believe that You sent Me." Now when He had said these things, He cried with a loud voice, "Lazarus, come forth!" And he who had died came out bound hand and foot with graveclothes, and his face was wrapped with a cloth. Jesus said to them, "Loose him, and let him go."

Then many of the Jews who had come to Mary, and had seen the things Jesus did, believed in Him. But some of them went away to the Pharisees and told them the things Jesus did. Then the chief priests and the Pharisees gathered a council and said, "What shall we do? For this Man works many signs. If we let Him alone like this, everyone will believe in Him, and the Romans will come and take away both our place and nation."

And one of them, Caiaphas, being high priest that year, said to them, "You know nothing at all, nor do you consider that it is expedient for us that one man should die for the people, and not that the whole nation should perish." Now this he did not say on his own authority; but being high priest that year he prophesied that Jesus would die for the nation, and not for that nation only, but also that He would gather together in one the children of God who were scattered abroad.

Then, from that day on, they plotted to put Him to death. (John 11:38–53)

Caiaphas: High priest [from] c. AD 18 . . . until AD 36 when, along with Pontius Pilate, he was removed by the Romans. He took a leading part in the trial and condemnation of Jesus. (*MacArthur Bible Commentary*, page 1394)

13. This passage depicts Jesus raising His friend Lazarus from the dead. What different reactions did people have to the news of a man's return from the dead?

_____

_____

_____

_____

_____

14. Why do you think a resurrection didn't convince everyone who heard about it to become a follower of Jesus?

_____

_____

_____

_____

_____

The message of the cross is foolishness to those who are perishing, but to us who are being saved it is the power of God. (1 Corinthians 1:18)

15. How does this story underscore what Abraham says at the end of the parable about the rich man and the fictional Lazarus?

_____

_____

_____

_____

_____

_____

Explore the Key Points

Take some time to consider how some of the big ideas of this chapter intersect with your own life. It will be helpful to answer these questions on your own before you discuss them with your group. If you're meeting with a group, you may want to have someone read aloud the key point before you discuss it.

The Sufficiency of Scripture

At the end of the parable of the rich man and Lazarus, Abraham says, "If they do not hear Moses and the prophets, neither will they be persuaded though one rise from the dead" (Luke 16:31). The phrase "Moses and the prophets" is a way of referring to the thirty-nine books of the Old Testament, the whole of Scripture that was available in Jesus' day. Jesus is saying that the Word of God is powerfully sufficient to bring people to repentance if their hearts are open to hearing and understanding.

The reason the rich man's brothers were careless unbelievers in danger of hell was not because there was something missing in the words of Scripture that came to them week by week in the synagogue. There is no better method or more effective messenger with special power to give sight to the blind or life to the dead. There is no new style of ministry or strategy for evangelism that has superior power to overcome depravity and awaken a spiritually dead, self-centered, self-willed, hypocritical, religious sinner (or any other kind of sinner, for that matter). The power is in the Word of God.

*Like anyone steeped in **Pharisaical** religion, [the rich man's] only concern is about a few people in his **immediate** family. (Parables, page 171)*

The word of God is living and powerful. (Hebrews 4:12)

Faith: To relinquish trust in oneself and transfer that trust to someone or something else. (*MacArthur Bible Commentary*, page 1214)

As Paul wrote, "Faith comes by hearing, and hearing by the word of God" (Romans 10:17). The rich man was in hell not because he lacked information, but because he ignored the message he had received through the Word of God. The only way his brothers would ever escape hell would be by listening to that message and believing it.

Likewise, when we share the gospel with unbelievers today, we need to make the Word of God our primary resource. As Paul told the believers in Corinth, "When I came to you, I did not come with excellence of speech or of wisdom declaring to you the testimony of God. For I determined not to know anything among you except Jesus Christ and Him crucified. I was with you in weakness, in fear, and in much trembling. And my speech and my preaching were not with persuasive words of human wisdom, but in demonstration of the Spirit and of power, that your faith should not be in the wisdom of men but in the power of God" (1 Corinthians 2:1–5).

[The gospel] is the power of God to salvation for everyone who believes. (Romans 1:16)

Many people today have negative expectations about the Bible that can be dispelled if we sit down with them in a nonthreatening manner and just read the Gospels together.

16. Think of an unbeliever you know. What attitudes does that person have about the Bible?

_____

_____

_____

_____

_____

_____

The mystery which has been hidden from ages and from generations . . . has been revealed to His saints. (Colossians 1:26)

17. How could you go about getting an unbeliever interested in what the Bible says?

_____

_____

_____

_____

_____

18. Some Christians have doubts about Scripture's sufficiency in drawing someone to faith. What has been your experience? What role has the Word of God played in your own journey to faith?

_____

_____

_____

_____

_____

_____

_____

What Jesus Taught About Hell

In the Gospels, Jesus uses the word "hell" (*gehenna*) twelve times. This was the word the Jews of His day used for the place where the wicked would go after divine judgment. For example, Jesus says in the Sermon on the Mount, "You have heard that it was said to those of old, 'You shall not murder, and whoever murders will be in danger of the judgment.' But I say to you that whoever is angry with his brother without a cause shall be in danger of the judgment. And whoever says to his brother, 'Raca!' shall be in danger of the council. But whoever says, 'You fool!' shall be in danger of hell fire" (Matthew 5:21–22).

Clearly, in this passage hell (*gehenna*) fire is associated with the judgment of God. Likewise, in the parable of the sheep and the goats (see Matthew 25:31–46), Jesus predicts that He will sit on a throne and separate the righteous from the wicked. The righteous will inherit the kingdom, while the wicked will be sent "into the everlasting fire prepared for the devil and his angels" (verse 41).

The image of fire comes up again in the parable of the wheat and the tares. An enemy sows tares (a weed) in a farmer's field of wheat, but instead of trying to destroy the tares while they are small, the farmer waits until the wheat and tares are full grown. Then it is easy for him to tell them apart, tie the tares in bundles, and burn them. Jesus explains, "Therefore as the tares are gathered and burned in the fire, so it will be at the end of this age. The Son of Man will send out His angels, and they will gather out of His kingdom all things that offend, and those who practice lawlessness, and will cast them into the furnace of fire. There will be wailing and gnashing of teeth. Then the righteous will shine forth as the sun in the kingdom of their Father" (Matthew 13:40–43).

In all of these passages, Jesus associates hell with fire. Elsewhere He also associates it with darkness as well as weeping and the gnashing of teeth. He says in Matthew 8:11–12, "I say to you that many will come from east and west, and sit down with Abraham, Isaac, and Jacob in the kingdom of heaven. But the sons of the kingdom will be cast out into outer darkness. There will be weeping and gnashing of teeth." Darkness also appears in Matthew 22:13 and 25:30.

In summary, hell is a place of fire, darkness, and everlasting sorrow, and it is the destination of all who reject the lordship of Christ.

19. What emotions do "weeping and gnashing of teeth" convey?

_____

_____

_____

_____

_____

_____

Hell: A reference to the Hinnom Valley, southwest of Jerusalem. . . . In Jesus' day, it was a garbage dump where fires burned continually, aptly symbolizing eternal fire. (*MacArthur Bible Commentary*, page 1131)

Hades: All people who die go to Hades in the sense that death leads from the visible world to the invisible. . . . Unfortunately, many people mistakenly associate Hades with hell. (*MacArthur Bible Commentary*, page 2037)

Hell is **punitive**, not remedial. People in hell don't get **better**. . . . Hell **fixes** the destiny and the character of the **reprobate** forever. (*Parables*, page 170)

This is the condemnation, that the light has come into the world, and men loved darkness rather than light, because their deeds were evil. (John 3:19)

20. What aspects of hell does darkness convey?

_____

_____

_____

_____

_____

21. How do these images of hell affect you?

_____

_____

_____

_____

Living the Parable

We've covered a lot in this lesson. Now it is your chance to pull it all together and decide what is the most important principle(s) you need to take to heart. You probably can't change your life in half a dozen ways this week, so prayerfully consider what is God's top priority for you.

22. What is your main takeaway(s) from this lesson? What do you want to take to heart as you go forward?

_____

_____

_____

_____

23. What are some things you will do to apply what you've learned?

_____

_____

_____

_____

Reflect and Respond

Repentance: To turn from sin and [amend] one's life. (*Merriam-Webster*)

At the end of each lesson, you will find suggested Scripture readings for spending time alone with God during five days of the coming week. Each day of this week's readings will deal with the theme of repentance, because repentance and faith are the keys to escaping hell. Read each passage slowly, pausing to think about what is being said. Rather than approaching this as an assignment to complete, think of it as an encounter with your heavenly Father. Use any of the questions that are helpful.

Day 1

1. Read 1 John 1:8–10. Why is it self-deception to say we haven't sinned?

_____

_____

_____

_____

If we say that we have no sin, we deceive ourselves, and the truth is not in us. (1 John 1:8)

2. Why does it treat God as a liar to say we haven't sinned?

_____

_____

_____

_____

_____

3. What happens when we confess our sins?

_____

_____

_____

_____

If we confess our sins, He is faithful and just to forgive us our sins and to cleanse us from all unrighteousness. If we say that we have not sinned, we make Him a liar, and His word is not in us. (1 John 1:9–10)

4. Why is confession essential to repentance?

_____

_____

_____

_____

5. What, if anything, do you have to confess to the Lord today?

_____

_____

_____

_____

_____

Day 2

1. Read Luke 15:1–7. What situation motivated Jesus to tell this parable?

_____

_____

_____

The tax collectors and the sinners drew near to Him to hear Him. (Luke 15:1)

What man of you, having a hundred sheep, if he loses one of them, does not leave the ninety-nine in the wilderness, and go after the one which is lost until he finds it? And when he has found it, he lays it on his shoulders, rejoicing.
(Luke 15:4–5)

2. Why does the shepherd rejoice so much over the found sheep?

_____

_____

_____

3. Why does God rejoice so much over the repentant sinner?

_____

_____

_____

_____

_____

4. What point does Jesus make in the parable that is related to the situation that prompted it?

_____

_____

_____

_____

_____

I say to you that likewise there will be more joy in heaven over one sinner who repents than over ninety-nine just persons who need no repentance. (Luke 15:7)

5. Is repentance easier for you when you think about how much joy it brings to God? Explain.

_____

_____

_____

_____

_____

Day 3

When the Pharisees saw it, they said to His disciples, "Why does your Teacher eat with tax collectors and sinners?" (Matthew 9:11)

1. Read Matthew 9:9–13. How is this situation similar to the one depicted in Luke 15:1–2?

_____

_____

_____

_____

2. What does this similarity tell you about Jesus? About the Pharisees?

_____

_____

_____

_____

3. How does Jesus explain His actions this time?

_____
_____
_____
_____

When Jesus heard that, He said to them, "Those who are well have no need of a physician, but those who are sick." (Matthew 9:12)

4. Are you more likely to eat with the righteous or with the tax collectors and sinners? Why do you think that is the case?

_____
_____
_____
_____
_____

5. What do Jesus' words in verse 13 motivate you to do?

_____
_____
_____
_____

I did not come to call the righteous, but sinners, to repentance. (Matthew 9:13)

Day 4

1. Read Hosea 6:1–3. How does this passage convey an attitude of repentance?

_____
_____
_____
_____

Come, and let us return to the LORD; for He has torn, but He will heal us; He has stricken, but He will bind us up. After two days He will revive us; on the third day He will raise us up, that we may live in His sight. (Hosea 6:1–2)

2. What does this passage say the Lord will do if the people repent?

_____
_____
_____
_____
_____

3. What does "He will come to us like the rain" (verse 3) mean to people who live in a country plagued with drought?

_____
_____
_____
_____

4. How do you "pursue the knowledge of the Lord" (verse 3)?

_____

_____

_____

_____

_____

5. How does this passage affect you? Are you motivated to say or do anything?

_____

_____

_____

_____

_____

_____

Day 5

1. Read Psalm 51:1–17. What does the psalmist say about God that motivates him to repentance? Make a list of the things he says about God.

_____

_____

_____

_____

_____

2. Which of those things on your list would prompt someone—you, perhaps—to turn away from sin and turn toward God?

_____

_____

_____

_____

_____

_____

3. Why does the psalmist talk about God's response to repentance as washing, cleansing, and blotting out? What does this say about sin?

_____

_____

_____

_____

_____

4. How is it significant that the psalmist looks to God to create in him a new heart (see verse 10)? What does this mean? Why is it God's job?

_____

_____

_____

_____

_____

Create in me a clean heart, O God, and renew a steadfast spirit within me. Do not cast me away from Your presence, and do not take Your Holy Spirit from me. (Psalm 51:10–11)

5. What do you want to do in response to this psalm, if anything?

_____

_____

_____

_____

_____

_____

Prayer for the Week

Dear Lord, thank You that You respond so warmly to confession and repentance. Thank You that when I confess, You are faithful and just to forgive my sins and cleanse me from unrighteousness. Thank You that You rejoice when one lost sinner repents. Please give me Your heart for the lost, for the tax collectors and sinners. I want to reach out to them with Your generous offer of forgiveness and healing. I don't want to be one of the righteous who stands aloof from those in need of the gospel. If I have not been generous with the gospel in the past, please forgive me, cleanse me, and create in me a new heart. Have mercy on me according to Your lovingkindness. And have mercy on others through me. In our Lord Jesus' name. Amen. ☀

A Lesson About
Persistence in Prayer

He spoke a parable to them,
that men always ought to pray and not lose heart.

LUKE 18:1

Main Objectives

In this study, you will (1) look at reasons why we should pray for Jesus to return and bring justice to the earth, and (2) consider why we should pray for Jesus' return and get past the things of this world that tempt us to lose heart.

Read and Review

Read chapter 10 from *Parables* and answer the questions that follow. If you're meeting in a small group, you might want to have someone read each of the following excerpts from *Parables* aloud before you discuss the questions related to it.

Never Lose Heart

[The point of the parable of the persistent widow is that] "men always ought to pray and not lose heart" (Luke 18:1). No matter how bleak the times; even if all the world seems to be barreling toward doom and eternal judgment, righteous men and women must persist in prayer—and they can be confident that God will hear and answer His people.

Our **prayers** are not always answered speedily, on our preferred **timetable**. (*Parables*, page 176)

[The angels said,] "We will destroy this place, because the outcry against them has grown great before the face of the LORD."
(Genesis 19:13)

This is an encouragement for believers living in evil times, seeing the world grow more hostile, sensing the approach of judgment, feeling alone and isolated "as it was in the days of Noah" (17:26) and "as it was also in the days of Lot" (verse 28). In other words, this story has a particular application in times like ours. The days are evil. The need is critical. Our praying should be urgent, passionate, and persistent. We must not lose heart. (Parables, pages 177–178)

1. Why might we be tempted to "lose heart" when praying?

_____

_____

_____

_____

_____

_____

The wickedness of man was great in the earth. . . . The earth also was corrupt before God.
(Genesis 6:5, 11)

2. How are today's times like the days of Noah? (See Genesis 6:5, 11.)

_____

_____

_____

_____

_____

_____

3. What aspects of today's times look bleak to you? What aspects give you hope?

_____

_____

_____

_____

_____

_____

The Encouragement We Need

[Jesus] encouraged the disciples both to **watch** eagerly and to **wait** patiently for His return. Here He is **encouraging** them to pray faithfully until that day comes.
(*Parables*, page 184)

The difference between a long time and a short time is nothing in God's timing. "With the Lord one day is as a thousand years, and a thousand years as one day" (2 Peter 3:8). All history is a blink of the eye compared to eternity. But from our perspective, time often seems to drag. To this widow [in Luke 18:1–6], the time span between the injustice she suffered and the judge's final vindication probably seemed like an aeon. To the apostle John, when Jesus did not return in his lifetime, that must have seemed like an interminable delay. For believers nearly two thousand years later, Jesus' admonition "to pray and not lose heart" is just the encouragement we need.

Today, at a rapidly accelerating pace worldwide, the Word of God is mocked, vilified, and censured. Christians are routinely maligned, persecuted, and oppressed, even in supposedly advanced Western cultures. In the Middle East, Africa, and parts of Asia Christians live in constant danger of martyrdom. Even by the most conservative measure, thousands are killed every year for their faith.

We long for Christ to come back and put an end to ungodliness and oppression—destroying sin forever and establishing His kingdom in righteousness. Jesus Himself taught us to pray, "Thy kingdom come" (Luke 11:2 KJV). Here, He encourages us to pray that prayer relentlessly, and not to lose heart. (Parables, pages 184–185)

[Look] for the blessed hope and glorious appearing of our great God and Savior Jesus Christ. (Titus 2:13)

4. What gives you courage as you go to God in prayer?

_____

_____

_____

_____

_____

5. What, if anything, hinders you from praying boldly?

Let us therefore come boldly to the throne of grace. (Hebrews 4:16)

_____

_____

_____

_____

_____

6. What would help you persist in prayer for God's kingdom to come in its fullness?

Persistence: To continue doing something or trying to do something even though it is difficult or opposed by other people. (*Merriam-Webster*)

_____

_____

_____

_____

_____

Heart-Cry of the True Believer

It is impossible to live the Christian life faithfully unless it is in the light of the Second Coming. Knowing the end of the story gives us confidence and stability. As Paul says, "Be steadfast, immovable, always abounding in the work of the Lord, knowing that your labor is not in vain in the Lord" (1 Corinthians 15:58).

Jesus' question in Luke 18:8, "When the Son of Man comes, will He really find faith on the earth?" ought to provoke us to self-reflection. . . . Are we faithfully praying for His return? I suspect that if He were to come right now, He would find multitudes who call themselves Christians who are totally unprepared for Him, not particularly eager for Him to come, and too enthralled with this life and worldly values to think much about it.

That is the antithesis of real faith. The heart-cry of the true believer is Maranatha! *"O Lord, come!" (1 Corinthians 16:22). (Parables, page 187)*

Son of Man: [This title] serves both to emphasize the difference between God the Creator and His creatures. . . . Jesus adopted the title Son of Man because He, too, is a representative person—the "last Adam" who became a life-giving spirit. (*MacArthur Bible Commentary*, page 912)

JOHN MACARTHUR | PARABLES WORKBOOK

Our citizenship is in heaven, from which we also eagerly wait for the Savior, the Lord Jesus Christ. (Philippians 3:20)

7. Why is it impossible to live the Christian life faithfully except in light of the Second Coming?

_____

_____

_____

_____

_____

8. Do you have a habit of praying for Christ to return? Why or why not?

_____

_____

_____

_____

_____

_____

Wait on the LORD; be of good courage, and He shall strengthen your heart. (Psalm 27:14)

9. How eager are you for Christ to return? Is it something you think about a lot, or are you busy with what you have on your plate in this life?

_____

_____

_____

_____

_____

_____

Make the Connection

Read the following Scripture passages and answer the questions provided. If you are meeting in a small group, you might want to have someone read each passage aloud before you discuss the questions related to it.

What the judge would not do out of **compassion** for the widow or reverence for God, he would do out of **sheer frustration** with her incessant **pleading**. (*MacArthur Bible Commentary*, page 1316)

He spoke a parable to them, that men always ought to pray and not lose heart, saying: "There was in a certain city a judge who did not fear God nor regard man. Now there was a widow in that city; and she came to him, saying, 'Get justice for me from my adversary.' And he would not for a while; but afterward he said within himself, 'Though I do not fear God nor regard man, yet because this widow troubles me I will avenge her, lest by her continual coming she weary me.'"

Then the Lord said, "Hear what the unjust judge said. And shall God not avenge His own elect who cry out day and night to Him, though He bears long with them? I tell you that He will avenge them speedily. Nevertheless, when the Son of Man comes, will He really find faith on the earth?" (Luke 18:1–8)

10. How is God different from the judge in this parable?

_____
_____
_____
_____

God is light and in Him is no darkness at all. (1 John 1:5)

11. What does the difference between God and the judge have to do with the point of the parable?

_____
_____
_____
_____

12. How will God "avenge" the elect who cry out to Him?

_____
_____
_____
_____

Do not take revenge, my dear friends, but leave room for God's wrath. (Romans 12:19 NIV)

Then He said to the disciples, "The days will come when you will desire to see one of the days of the Son of Man, and you will not see it. And they will say to you, 'Look here!' or 'Look there!' Do not go after them or follow them. For as the lightning that flashes out of one part under heaven shines to the other part under heaven, so also the Son of Man will be in His day. But first He must suffer many things and be rejected by this generation. And as it was in the days of Noah, so it will be also in the days of the Son of Man: They ate, they drank, they married wives, they were given in marriage, until the day that Noah entered the ark, and the flood came and destroyed them all. Likewise as it was also in the days of Lot: They ate, they drank, they bought, they sold, they planted, they built; but on the day that Lot went out of Sodom it rained fire and brimstone from heaven and destroyed them all. Even so will it be in the day when the Son of Man is revealed.

"In that day, he who is on the housetop, and his goods are in the house, let him not come down to take them away. And likewise the one who is in the field, let him not turn back. Remember Lot's wife. Whoever seeks to save his life will lose it, and whoever loses his life will preserve it. I tell you, in that night there will be two men in one bed: the one will be taken and the other will be left. Two women will be grinding together: the one will be taken and the other left. Two men will be in the field: the one will be taken and the other left."

And they answered and said to Him, "Where, Lord?"

So He said to them, "Wherever the body is, there the eagles will be gathered together." (Luke 17:22–37)

Jesus taught the disciples that His coming was **imminent**—meaning that He *could* return at any time. On the other hand, He might come **later** than anyone expects. During His earthly ministry, even Jesus Himself, in the scope of His **finite** human consciousness, did not **know** the precise timetable. (*Parables*, page 184)

Lot's wife: Her attachment to Sodom was so powerful that she delayed and looked back; she was overwhelmed by oncoming judgment. (*MacArthur Bible Commentary*, page 1315)

*We shall all be changed—
in a moment, in the twinkling of
an eye, at the last trumpet.*
(1 Corinthians 15:51–52)

13. This passage provides the immediate context for the parable. How will the Second Coming of Christ (the Son of Man) be like lightning?

_____

_____

_____

_____

_____

_____

_____

14. How will the Second Coming be like the days of Noah and Lot?

_____

_____

_____

_____

_____

_____

*Luke 17 . . . is dominated
by warnings of **doom** and
sudden **disaster**, culminating
in a gruesome image of
death and **corruption**.*
(Parables, page 177)

15. What light does this passage shed on the context of the parable in Luke 18:1–8?

_____

_____

_____

_____

_____

_____

Explore the Key Points

Take some time to consider how some of the big ideas of this chapter intersect with your own life. It will be helpful to answer these questions on your own before you discuss them with your group. If you're meeting with a group, you may want to have someone read aloud the key point before you discuss it.

Events Around the Second Coming

Scripture depicts a series of events leading up to and following the Second Coming of Christ. The first event we look forward to is Christ's return for His church before executing judgment on the ungodly (see Luke 17:34–36; 1 Thessalonians 4:15–18). Those believers who have died will be raised bodily from the dead, and those who are still alive when Christ comes will be caught up to meet them in the air. They will all be taken to heaven together, and their union with Christ will never end. Christ will not come to earth at this time; believers will go to Him.

*The dead in Christ will rise first.
Then we who are alive and remain
shall be caught up together with
them in the clouds to meet the Lord.*
(1 Thessalonians 4:16–17)

Once all true Christians have been taken from the earth, there will be a seven-year time of tribulation on earth. God will unleash His wrath on the wicked in judgments described in detail in Revelation 6–19. Many people will resist God even then, but many also will come to faith in Christ. This number includes many Jews, who will reestablish Jerusalem as a center of true worship of God and Christ.

At the end of the seven years, Christ and the church will return to earth to do battle with the ungodly, defeat them, and establish His thousand-year reign on earth (see Revelation 20:1–10). All those who survive the judgments up to this point will be believers, so initially the thousand-year-reign (the millennium) will be for believers only. But some people born during this golden age will reject Christ's rule, and at the end of the thousand years, Satan will be released to lead a brief rebellion against Christ. The Lord will quickly defeat Satan and will condemn him and his angels permanently. God will then recreate a new heavens and a new earth, where His people will live in joy forever.

16. How does it affect you to think about these events? What feelings does it evoke?

_____

_____

_____

_____

_____

17. Why is it important that God will remove His church from the earth before the worst of the judgments fall?

_____

_____

_____

_____

18. What about these final events is ultimately good news for you?

_____

_____

_____

_____

> **Tribulation:** Immediately following the removal of the church from the earth, the righteous judgments of God will be poured out upon an unbelieving world . . . these judgments will be climaxed by the return of Christ in glory to the earth. (*MacArthur Bible Commentary*, page xviii)

> *God will wipe away every tear from their eyes; there shall be no more death, nor sorrow, nor crying.* (Revelation 21:4)

Persistent Prayer

Although the parable of the persistent widow is primarily about God's faithfulness to answer our prayers for Christ's return in justice, it is one passage of Scripture among many that assure us God answers persistent prayer:

The effective, fervent prayer of a righteous man avails much. (James 5:16)

Ask, and it will be given to you; seek, and you will find; knock, and it will be opened to you. For everyone who asks receives, and he who seeks finds, and to him who knocks it will be opened. Or what man is there among you who, if his son asks for bread, will give him a stone? Or if he asks for a fish, will he give him a serpent? If you then, being evil, know how to give good gifts to your children, how much more will your Father who is in heaven give good things to those who ask Him! (Matthew 7:7–11)

Whatever things you ask in prayer, believing, you will receive. (Matthew 21:22)

This is the confidence that we have in Him, that if we ask anything according to His will, He hears us. And if we know that He hears us, whatever we ask, we know that we have the petitions that we have asked of Him. (1 John 5:14–15)

God will never give us stones when we ask for bread. Yet for reasons that are supremely wise, and gracious, and right—but often unknown and unexplained to us—God sometimes delays in answering our prayers. Yet He encourages us to keep praying with persistence and passion, never losing faith and not growing faint.

19. How does it benefit us to have to keep praying with persistence and passion instead of getting answers to our prayers right away?

_____

_____

_____

_____

_____

_____

20. What is something you have been praying about for a long time without receiving what you've been asking for?

_____

_____

_____

_____

_____

_____

_____

*"Even so, **come**, Lord Jesus!" That prayer ought to be on our lips **perpetually**. And those hopes should **govern** all our thoughts. That is Jesus' **point** in the parable of the unjust judge. (Parables, page 188)*

Continue earnestly in prayer, being vigilant in it with thanksgiving. (Colossians 4:2)

21. In Hebrews 11:13, the writer looks back at Abraham, Sarah, and other faithful followers and notes, "These all died in faith, not having received the promises, but having seen them afar off were assured of them, embraced them and confessed that they were strangers and pilgrims on the earth." Are you willing to die in faith, not having yet received what God has promised you? Why or why not?

Because you have seen Me, you have believed. Blessed are those who have not seen and yet have believed. (John 20:29)

_____

_____

_____

_____

_____

_____

Living the Parable

We've covered a lot in this lesson. Now it is your chance to pull it all together and decide what is the most important principle(s) you need to take to heart. You probably can't change your life in half a dozen ways this week, so prayerfully consider what is God's top priority for you.

22. What is your main takeaway(s) from this lesson? What do you want to take to heart as you go forward?

_____

_____

_____

_____

_____

23. What are some things you will do to apply what you've learned?

_____

_____

_____

_____

_____

_____

Reflect and Respond

At the end of each lesson, you will find suggested Scripture readings for spending time alone with God during five days of the coming week. Each day of this week's readings will deal with the theme of prayer. Read each passage slowly, pausing to think about what is being said. Rather than approaching this as an assignment to complete, think of it as an encounter with your heavenly Father. Use any of the questions that are helpful.

Man's **faith** and **prayer** must be consistent with God's sovereignty. (_MacArthur Bible Commentary_, page 1239)

Day 1

When you pray, you shall not be like the hypocrites. For they love to pray standing in the synagogues and on the corners of the streets, that they may be seen by men. (Matthew 6:5)

1. Read Matthew 6:5–8. What motivation for prayer does Jesus urge us *not* to have in verse 5?

_____

_____

_____

_____

_____

Pray to your Father who is in the secret place; and your Father who sees in secret will reward you openly. (Matthew 6:6)

2. What is a good motivation for prayer?

_____

_____

_____

_____

Do not use vain repetitions as the heathen do. For they think that they will be heard for their many words. (Matthew 6:7)

3. What are "vain repetitions" (verse 7)? What is wrong with this type of prayer?

_____

_____

_____

_____

_____

_____

4. Why is private prayer so important in addition to the praying we do in groups?

_____

_____

_____

_____

_____

_____

Your Father knows the things you have need of before you ask Him. (Matthew 6:8)

5. Do you pray on your own on a daily basis? What motivates you? What gets in the way?

_____

_____

_____

_____

_____

Day 2

1. Read Matthew 6:9–13. What priorities for prayer does Jesus offer in this outline? What should we pray about?

_____
_____
_____
_____
_____

2. What does "hallowed be Your name" mean (verse 9)? Why is this an important declaration for us to make?

_____
_____
_____
_____
_____
_____

Our Father in heaven, hallowed be Your name. (Matthew 6:9)

3. Why do we pray for God's kingdom to come (see verse 10)? How is this related to what we learned from Luke 18:1–8?

_____
_____
_____
_____
_____
_____

Your kingdom come. Your will be done on earth as it is in heaven. (Matthew 6:10)

4. Why do we pray for "daily bread" (verse 11), even though God knows we need it?

_____
_____
_____
_____
_____
_____

Give us this day our daily bread. (Matthew 6:11)

5. Are there any topics in this prayer for which you don't consistently pray? If so, which ones? How can Jesus' words in this passage enrich your prayer life?

_____
_____
_____
_____
_____
_____
_____

Do not lead us into temptation, but deliver us from the evil one. For Yours is the kingdom and the power and the glory forever. (Matthew 6:13)

Day 3

"Lend me three loaves; for a friend of mine has come to me on his journey, and I have nothing to set before him." (Luke 11:5–6)

1. Read Luke 11:5–8. In this parable, what is the situation that prompts the person to go out at midnight and ask the friend for help?

_____

_____

_____

_____

"Do not trouble me; the door is now shut, and my children are with me in bed; I cannot rise and give to you." (Luke 11:7)

2. How does the friend respond to the request?

_____

_____

_____

_____

3. How is God like and unlike the friend who is asked for help?

_____

_____

_____

_____

Though he will not rise and give to him because he is his friend, yet because of his persistence he will rise and give him as many as he needs. (Luke 11:8)

4. Does it ever seem to you that God is saying, "I'm busy, I'm in bed, go away"? What can give a person that impression?

_____

_____

_____

5. What do you need to ask God for persistently?

_____

_____

_____

_____

Day 4

He who abides in Me, and I in him, bears much fruit; for without Me you can do nothing. (John 15:5)

1. Read John 15:5–10. What does it mean to "abide" in Christ?

_____

_____

_____

_____

2. How is abiding linked to answered prayer in verse 7?

_____

_____

_____

_____

I am the vine, you are the branches.
(John 15:5)

3. Do you experience the reality of being a "branch" connected to a "vine"? If so, what is that like? If not, what's missing?

_____

_____

_____

_____

_____

_____

If you abide in Me, and
My words abide in you,
you will ask what you desire,
and it shall be done for you.
(John 15:7)

4. What does it mean to have Christ's words abide in you (see verse 7)?

_____

_____

_____

_____

_____

5. How is keeping Christ's commandments related to abiding in Him (see verse 10)?

_____

_____

_____

_____

_____

If you keep My commandments,
you will abide in My love,
just as I have kept My Father's
commandments and abide
in His love. (John 15:10)

Day 5

1. Read Ephesians 3:13–19. Paul is writing these words from prison, and in verse 13 he asks his readers not to lose heart because of the tribulations he is suffering. Why might knowing that their mentor is in prison cause his friends in Ephesus to lose heart?

_____

_____

_____

_____

_____

Therefore I ask that you do not lose
heart at my tribulations for you,
which is your glory. For this reason
I bow my knees to the Father of our
Lord Jesus Christ, from whom the
whole family in heaven and earth is
named. (Ephesians 3:13–15)

2. Paul's prayer is meant to encourage them so that they don't lose heart. What does he ask for?

_____

_____

_____

_____

_____

_____

_____

3. How might this prayer encourage someone not to lose heart?

_____

_____

_____

_____

_____

[I pray] that He would grant you, according to the riches of His glory, to be strengthened with might through His Spirit in the inner man, that Christ may dwell in your hearts through faith; that you, being rooted and grounded in love, may be able to comprehend with all the saints what is the width and length and depth and height— to know the love of Christ which passes knowledge; that you may be filled with all the fullness of God.
(Ephesians 3:16–19)

4. What does it mean to be "strengthened with might through His Spirit in the inner man" (verse 16)?

_____

_____

_____

_____

_____

5. Which one of Paul's requests do you most need to pray for persistently?

_____

_____

_____

_____

_____

_____

Prayer for the Week

Dear Lord, thank You for being our loving Father and for hearing the prayers we offer in secret. Thank You that You desire relationship with us, and that You want to hear the desires of our hearts even though You know what we need and want. Teach us to pray fervently for the things that matter to You. We want Your kingdom to come and Your will to be done on earth. Please come speedily to bring the fullness of Your kingdom. We know You're not like the friend in the parable who says, "Don't trouble me." You are a God who rewards persistence, and we're grateful for that. Strengthen us through Your Spirit. Root us in Your love. Teach us to abide in You daily, hourly. In our Lord Jesus' name. Amen. ✳

A Lesson About
God's Love

"Bring out the best robe and put it on him, and put a ring on his hand and sandals on his feet. And bring the fatted calf here and kill it, and let us eat and be merry; for this my son was dead and is alive again; he was lost and is found." And they began to be merry.

LUKE 15:22-24

Main Objectives

In this lesson, you will look at the parable of the prodigal son found in Luke 15:11–32 and focus on its three main characters: (1) the prodigal, who committed shameful deeds against his father; (2) the father, who extended forgiveness to his wayward son; and (3) the older brother, whose selfishness and self-righteousness prevented him from extending grace to his family members.

Read and Review

Read each of the excerpts in this lesson from *The Prodigal Son* and answer the questions that follow. If you're meeting in a small group, you might want to have someone read each of the excerpts aloud before you discuss the questions related to it.

The Prodigal

The picture Jesus paints is of a young man, who is apparently not yet married— because he wants to go and sow his wild oats. He was probably in his teens and

Of all Jesus' parables, this one is the most **richly** detailed, **powerfully** dramatic, and intensely **personal**. (*Prodigal Son*, page xii)

The land shall not be sold permanently, for the land is Mine; for you are strangers and sojourners with Me. And in all the land of your possession you shall grant redemption of the land. (Leviticus 25:23–24)

There is a way that seems right to a man, but its end is the way of death. (Proverbs 16:25)

Unless you repent you will all likewise perish. (Luke 13:3)

obviously filled with shameless disrespect toward his father. His request for an early inheritance reveals how passionately deep-seated and wickedly hard-hearted his defiance was. Anyone acquainted with Middle Eastern culture would instantly see this (and most would find it repugnant in the extreme) because everything about the demand the boy made cut against the grain of Hebrew society's core values.

To begin with, the younger son's attitude regarding his inheritance was entirely inappropriate. From the earliest days of Israel, the laws governing the passage of family estates from generation to generation were among the most important and most distinctive cultural principles codified in the law of Moses. Family lands and possessions were not to be sold or transferred out of the family line. In dire cases where land had to be sold to avoid a disastrous bankruptcy, the Law even had a provision that guaranteed the eventual return of that property to its rightful family during the year of Jubilee (Leviticus 25:23–34). . . .

It is patently obvious that the younger son in Jesus' parable had not an ounce of gratitude in his heart for the legacy that generations of his family had provided for his father—and one day for him. He lacked both patience and discipline. Worst of all, by all appearances, he lacked any authentic love for his father.

This was perhaps the most disturbing aspect of the Prodigal Son's behavior. For a son in that culture to request his inheritance early was tantamount to saying, "Dad, I wish you were dead. You are in the way of my plans. You are a barrier. I want my freedom. I want my fulfillment. And I want out of this family now. I have other plans that don't involve you; they don't involve this family; they don't involve this estate; they don't even involve this village. I want nothing to do with any of you. Give me my inheritance now, and I am out of here." . . .

The Prodigal certainly did not find the kind of life he wanted when he began his escapade. All the glitter was off the gold in the far country. The road he had chosen to follow turned out to be an expressway to destruction. His freewheeling lifestyle had suddenly morphed into a terrible, crushing bondage. All his dreams had become nightmares. All his pleasure had turned to pain. All his fun had given way to profound sorrow. And this heedless young rebel who threw everything away for a few moments of self-indulgence was now forced into a lifestyle of utter self-deprivation. The revelry had ended. The laughs had been silenced. The music had stopped playing. His so-called friends were all gone. It was as bad as it could get, and he was about to die. . . .

At last, however, just when all hope for the younger brother would seem to be extinguished, "he came to himself." He woke up to reality. In the solitude of the pig fields, he was forced to face what he had become, and that somehow jolted him out of utter insensibility. Suddenly, he began to think clearly. His first instinct upon regaining his senses was to plan how he might get back to his father and his home. With all his resources spent and all his companions gone, he had nowhere else to go and no other means by which to survive. He was truly at the end of the road.

So for the first time in his life, the younger son was determined to walk away from his sin, plead for his father's forgiveness, and submit to his father's authority. He turned and headed home. (*The Prodigal Son*, pages 43–45, 69, 83)

1. What was the younger son's attitude toward his inheritance? Why was this so inappropriate for the culture of his time?

_____

_____

_____

_____

_____

2. What did the prodigal son discover once he was away from his father's care? What caused him to realize the truth of his situation and seek to change?

_____

_____

_____

_____

_____

Prodigal: Characterized by profuse or wasteful expenditure. (*Merriam-Webster*)

3. The younger son is not just a picture of the *worst* of sinners but *every* unredeemed sinner—including us. What does Paul tell us about our condition in Ephesians 2:12?

_____

_____

_____

_____

_____

You were without Christ, being aliens from the commonwealth of Israel and strangers from the covenants of promise, having no hope and without God in the world. (Ephesians 2:12)

The Father

The father would most likely [be expected to] meet [the prodigal son] with a measure of frigid indifference. To save face, the father would need to approach the arrangement formally, like a business deal, without showing any overt affection or tenderness for the boy. There was no negotiation to be done; the father would simply outline the terms of employment—spelling out what would be required of the boy, what kind of labor he could expect to be assigned, and how long he needed to serve before he could be given even the smallest measure of privilege. . . .

At this point, Jesus' parable suddenly took another dramatic and unexpected turn. Here was a father not merely willing to grant a measure of mercy in return for the promise of a lifetime of meritorious service—but eager to forgive freely, completely, at the very first sign of repentance: "When he was still a great way off, his father saw him and had compassion, and ran and fell on his neck and kissed him" (Luke 15:20).

It is evident that the father was looking diligently for the Prodigal's return. How else could he have seen him while he was still a long way off? We can safely imagine that the father had been looking steadily, scanning the horizon daily, repeatedly, for signs of the boy's return. He had been at it a long time too—probably since long before the initial shock of the boy's departure had even worn off. . . .

The father pictures **God**, eager to **forgive**, and longing for the return of the sinner. The main feature, however . . . is the **joy** of God, plus the celebrations that **fill heaven** when a sinner repents. (*MacArthur Bible Commentary*, page 1309)

You will seek Me and find Me, when you search for Me with all your heart. (Jeremiah 29:13)

The father's compassion was not merely sorrow over his son's past sin. Nor was it only a momentary sympathy prompted by the boy's present filthiness. (Remember, the Prodigal was by now in rags and smelled like pigs.) Certainly the father's feeling toward the son included a deep sense of pity over all the terrible things sin had already done to him. But it seems obvious that something else was amplifying the father's anguish at that precise moment. His action of running toward the son and intercepting him on the road suggests he had something terribly urgent and immediate on his mind. That's why I am convinced that what moved the father to run was a deep sense of empathy in anticipation of the contempt that was sure to be poured on the son as he walked through the village. The father took off in a sprint in order to be the first person to reach him, so that he could deflect the abuse he knew the boy would suffer. . . .

The Prodigal had come home prepared to kiss his father's feet. Instead, the father was kissing the Prodigal's pig-stinking head. . . . What a beautiful picture this is of the forgiveness offered in the gospel! The typical sinner wants out of the morass of sin, and his first instinct is to devise a plan. He will work off his guilt. He will reform himself. But such a plan could never succeed. The debt is too great to repay, and the sinner is helpless to change his own status. He is fallen, and he cannot alter that fact. So the Savior intercepts him. Christ has already run the gauntlet, taken the shame for himself, suffered the rebukes, borne the cruel taunts, and paid the price of the guilt in full. He embraces the sinner, pours out love upon him, grants complete forgiveness, and reconciles him to God. (The Prodigal Son, pages 110–111, 115, 117)

4. What would have been so shocking to Jesus' listeners about the father's reaction to his son's return? What would have been expected in that culture?

_____

_____

_____

_____

_____

_____

_____

_____

5. What does the fact the father was looking for the prodigal son daily tell us about his love for him? What does it tell us about God's love for us?

_____

_____

_____

_____

_____

_____

6. Why did the father run to meet his son? How does our Father run to us when we seek Him in repentance?

_____

_____

_____

_____

_____

_____

Draw near to God and He will draw near to you. (James 4:8)

The Elder Brother

The elder son is the third major character in the parable, and as it turns out, he is the one who embodies the parable's main lesson. His most obvious characteristic is his resentment for his younger brother. But underneath that, and even more ominously, it is clear that he has been nurturing a quietly smoldering hatred for the father—for a long, long time, it appears. This secretly rebellious spirit has shaped and molded his character in a most disturbing way. . . .

*The elder son has **never** truly been devoted to his father. He is by no means symbolic of the true believer. Instead, he depicts the religious hypocrite. He is the Pharisee figure in Jesus' story. He probably had the whole village sincerely believing that he was the "good" son—very respectful and faithful to his father. He stuck around the house. He pretended to be a loyal son. But in reality, he had no genuine respect for his father, no interest in what pleased his father, no love for the father's values, and no concern for his needy younger brother. That all becomes very clear as the story unfolds. . . .*

Just as the younger son's fleeing to the far country serves to show how poorly he regarded his father, so this one's being out in the field is a fitting metaphor for where he stood in terms of his own family. Both sons were far away from the father. In the end they both came home—but with totally different attitudes and to very different receptions. . . .

In the end, the firstborn son was in the very same place the younger son had started out. He wanted what he considered rightfully his, on his own terms, so that he could live however he pleased. He just had a different way of getting to that long-term goal. He lacked the boldness of his younger brother. He didn't have the moxie to run away. It was much easier for him just to wait until the father died, and then he would have what he wanted. (The Prodigal Son, pages 149–150, 155, 177)

The **elder brother** illustrates the wickedness of the Pharisees' **self-righteousness**, **prejudice**, and **indifference** toward repenting sinners. (*MacArthur Bible Commentary*, page 1309)

Hypocrite: A person who acts in contradiction to his or her stated beliefs or feelings. (*Merriam-Webster*)

The elder brother's attitude is a powerful **warning**, showing how easily and how subtly **unbelief** can masquerade as faithfulness. (*Prodigal Son*, page xviii)

7. Why does the elder brother embody the main lesson of the parable? Who does he depict in Jesus' day? Who does he represent in our day?

_____

_____

_____

_____

_____

_____

[The elder son] is a **sinner** who thinks hypocrisy is as good as real **righteousness**. What he looks like on the **outside** cloaks a seething rebellion on the **inside**. (*Prodigal Son*, page 149)

8. What in the parable reveals that the elder son resented his father? Why is it significant that he was out in the field when the celebration for the younger son took place?

_____

_____

_____

_____

_____

_____

9. In what ways were the attitudes of the younger son and older son similar? What was different in the way the elder son sought out his goals?

_____

_____

_____

_____

_____

Make the Connection

Read the following Scripture passages and answer the questions provided. If you are meeting in a small group, you might want to have someone read each passage aloud before you discuss the questions related to it.

The prodigal son evidently took his share in **liquid assets**, and left, abandoning his father, and heading into a life of **iniquity**. (*MacArthur Bible Commentary*, page 1310)

Then [Jesus] said: "A certain man had two sons. And the younger of them said to his father, 'Father, give me the portion of goods that falls to me.' So he divided to them his livelihood. And not many days after, the younger son gathered all together, journeyed to a far country, and there wasted his possessions with prodigal living. But when he had spent all, there arose a severe famine in that land, and he began to be in want. Then he went and joined himself to a citizen of that country, and he sent him into his fields to feed swine. And he would gladly have filled his stomach with the pods that the swine ate, and no one gave him anything.

"But when he came to himself, he said, 'How many of my father's hired servants have bread enough and to spare, and I perish with hunger! I will arise and go to my father, and will say to him, "Father, I have sinned against heaven and before you, and I am no longer worthy to be called your son. Make me like one of your hired servants."'

"And he arose and came to his father. But when he was still a great way off, his father saw him and had compassion, and ran and fell on his neck and kissed him. And the son said to him, 'Father, I have sinned against heaven and in your sight, and am no longer worthy to be called your son.'

[God] is not **indifferent** or **hostile**, but a Savior by nature longing to see sinners **repent**. (*MacArthur Bible Commentary*, page 1310)

"But the father said to his servants, 'Bring out the best robe and put it on him, and put a ring on his hand and sandals on his feet. And bring the fatted calf here and kill it, and let us eat and be merry; for this my son was dead and is alive again; he was lost and is found.' And they began to be merry." (Luke 15:11–24)

Fatted calf: A sacrifice or a feast of great celebration. (*MacArthur Bible Commentary*, page 1310)

10. What do you think drove the younger son to rebel against his father? What causes people today to rebel against their heavenly Father?

_____

_____

_____

_____

_____

11. What caused the young man to come to his senses? What was his plan to reconcile with his father after the terrible acts he had committed?

_____

_____

_____

_____

_____

The son did not get to finish his **rehearsed words** of repentance before the father **interrupted** to grant forgiveness. (*MacArthur Bible Commentary*, page 1310)

12. What was the father's plan for reconciling with his youngest son? How was that different from the prodigal son's plan?

_____

_____

_____

_____

_____

[*Jesus said,*] *"Now his older son was in the field. And as he came and drew near to the house, he heard music and dancing. So he called one of the servants and asked what these things meant. And he said to him, 'Your brother has come, and because he has received him safe and sound, your father has killed the fatted calf.'*

"But he was angry and would not go in. Therefore his father came out and pleaded with him. So he answered and said to his father, 'Lo, these many years I have been serving you; I never transgressed your commandment at any time; and yet you never gave me a young goat, that I might make merry with my friends. But as soon as this son of yours came, who has devoured your livelihood with harlots, you killed the fatted calf for him.'

"And he said to him, 'Son, you are always with me, and all that I have is yours. It was right that we should make merry and be glad, for your brother was dead and is alive again, and was lost and is found.'" (Luke 15:25–32)

Here was the **biggest event** the village had ever seen— the **greatest celebration** his family had ever hosted— and he knew **nothing** about it. (*Prodigal Son*, page 153)

Surely I am with you always. (Matthew 28:20 NIV)

151

13. Why wasn't the older son aware of the celebration? What does that tell us about his relationship with his father?

_____

_____

_____

_____

Grace: Signifies divine favor or goodwill, but it also means "that which gives joy" and "that which is a free gift." (*MacArthur Bible Commentary*, page 1444)

14. How did the father extend grace and show love to his eldest son?

_____

_____

_____

_____

15. What reasons did the older brother give for why he was angry? Why was he unable to extend grace to his younger brother who had returned home?

_____

_____

_____

_____

_____

_____

Explore the Key Points

Take some time to consider how some of the big ideas of this chapter intersect with your own life. It will be helpful to answer these questions on your own before you discuss them with your group. If you're meeting with a group, you may want to have someone read aloud the key point before you discuss it.

Distance from the Father

God sets the solitary in families; He brings out those who are bound into prosperity; but the rebellious dwell in a dry land. (Psalm 68:6)

The parable of the prodigal son gives us key insights into how the state of people's hearts affects their relationship with God. Sometimes, it is obvious when people have distanced themselves from God, because their words and actions illustrate the rebellious attitude of their hearts. In the parable, this type of sinner is represented by the younger son, who did not try to hide his disrespect for his father and the legacy his inheritance symbolized. For many of us, this describes a leg of our own faith journey. We belligerently claimed that God was dead and walked away from all that reminded us of him. We chased our own desires, made our own rules, and, for a time, found excitement in being our own masters.

But sometimes, it is not as obvious when people have distanced themselves from God. In the parable, the older son went through the motions of being "good" on the outside, but his interior motives were always to collect his inheritance. We can be like the older son. We fail to seek a loving relationship with the Father and selfishly expect the benefits, or blessings, to which we think we are entitled. We go to church, write our tithe checks, and behave in public. But we do not participate in the things that bring the Father joy or spend time with Him. Those who recognize their need for the Father are able to enjoy His presence as He meets with them and closes the distance between them.

In 1 Samuel 16:7, the Lord explained to the prophet Samuel how He judges a person: "Do not look at his appearance or at his physical stature, because I have refused him. For the LORD does not see as man sees; for man looks at the outward appearance, but the LORD looks at the heart." The younger son would have been despised as an outcast and recognized for his sinfulness, but the older brother would have been esteemed for his apparent faithful service. Jesus said that those who seek the honor of people and rely on their own self-righteousness "have their reward" (Matthew 6:2), which does not include closeness with God.

16. Why is it so difficult for people who think they are doing "good enough" in God's eyes to recognize their distance from God?

_____

_____

_____

_____

_____

_____

17. What are some signs that we have distanced ourselves from our heavenly Father?

_____

_____

_____

_____

_____

_____

18. Why are we often tempted to judge people based on outward appearances?

_____

_____

_____

_____

_____

_____

> The truth is, [the older son] didn't really even **believe** in grace. . . . The very idea of free forgiveness was **repugnant** to him. (*Prodigal Son*, page 161)

> *The law was given through Moses, but grace and truth came through Jesus Christ.* (John 1:17)

> *Do not judge according to appearance, but judge with righteous judgment.* (John 7:24)

The Father's Urgent Search

God's response to the repentant heart is exemplified in the parable by the father's urgency in being the first to reach his younger son and his eagerness to restore him publically. "The Son of Man came to seek and to save the lost" (Luke 19:10 NIV). This is the Father's purpose in sending Jesus to us. He is actively searching for the lost, just as the father was scanning the horizon for the son who had turned away from him.

The father also reached out to his older son and invited him to share his joy. The older son was just as lost, and the father sought to draw him close. But the older son's heart was not soft, fertile ground ready to accept the father's love. This reveals that when we feel God is far from us, it is not because He has left us or doesn't care, but because we don't see Him watching for us to turn to Him. The repentant heart is a beautiful thing in God's eyes: "There will be more rejoicing in heaven over one sinner who repents than over ninety-nine righteous persons who do not need to repent" (Luke 15:7 NIV). Our heavenly Father does not force Himself on an unwilling heart, but He does celebrate every heart that receives His love.

Paul writes, "You He made alive, who were dead in trespasses and sins, in which you once walked according to the course of this world. . . . But God, who is rich in mercy, because of His great love with which He loved us, even when we were dead in trespasses, made us alive together with Christ (by grace you have been saved)" (Ephesians 2:1–2, 4–5). The Father's love is great, rich in mercy, and gives life to the sinner. It takes a life that is dead and buried in sin and raises it up—clean, with a robe of honor, a ring of authority, and sandals reserved for a son.

> The **Pharisees** and **scribes** . . . spent their lives dealing with Scripture and **public** worship—but they never really possessed any of the **treasures** enjoyed by the repentant sinner. (*MacArthur Bible Commentary*, page 1311)

> He who received seed on the good ground is he who hears the word and understands it. (Matthew 13:23)

19. Review the parable of the soils in Matthew 13:18–23. What about the older son's character indicates his heart was not fertile soil?

_____

_____

_____

_____

_____

_____

> Behold, I stand at the door and knock. If anyone hears My voice and opens the door, I will come in to him and dine with him, and he with Me. (Revelation 3:20)

20. Read Revelation 3:20. What does Jesus promise to do when we answer the Father's urgent call?

_____

_____

_____

_____

_____

_____

21. Read 1 John 4:19–20. What does John say about the way we show our love for God? What does that love compel us to do?

_____

_____

_____

_____

_____

_____

If someone says, "I love God," and hates his brother, he is a liar; for he who does not love his brother whom he has seen, how can he love God whom he has not seen? (1 John 4:20)

Living the Parable

We've covered a lot in this lesson. Now it is your chance to pull it all together and decide what is the most important principle(s) you need to take to heart. You probably can't change your life in half a dozen ways this week, so prayerfully consider what is God's top priority for you.

22. What is your main takeaway(s) from this lesson? What do you want to take to heart as you go forward?

_____

_____

_____

_____

_____

_____

23. What are some things you will do to apply what you've learned?

_____

_____

_____

_____

_____

_____

Reflect and Respond

At the end of each lesson, you will find suggested Scripture readings for spending time alone with God during five days of the coming week. Each day of this week's readings will deal with the theme of our need for God's love, grace, and mercy, as demonstrated in the story of the prodigal son. Read each passage slowly, pausing to think about what is being said. Rather than approaching this as an assignment to complete, think of it as an encounter with your heavenly Father. Use any of the questions that are helpful.

The **invitation** to be part of the great celebratory banquet is still **open** to **all**. (*Prodigal Son*, page 198)

Day 1

He went to the Pharisee's house. . . . And behold, a woman in the city who was a sinner, when she knew that Jesus sat at the table in the Pharisee's house, brought an alabaster flask of fragrant oil.
(Luke 7:36–37)

1. Read Luke 7:36–39. In Jesus' parable of the prodigal son, the younger son represents the "extreme" type of sinner—the one who is openly rebellious toward God. How does Luke let us know the woman who met with Jesus is this type of person?

_____

_____

_____

_____

2. In Jesus' day, needy people could visit such banquets to receive leftovers. How did the woman take advantage of this custom? What drove her to seek Jesus?

_____

_____

_____

_____

3. What does the fact that the woman was willing to go to a Pharisee's house tell us about the level of her desperation?

_____

_____

_____

_____

_____

[She] stood at His feet behind Him weeping; and she began to wash His feet with her tears.
(Luke 7:38)

4. Why do you think Jesus allowed the woman to wash His feet and anoint them with oil?

_____

_____

_____

_____

He spoke to himself, saying, "This Man, if He were a prophet, would know who and what manner of woman this is who is touching Him, for she is a sinner."
(Luke 7:39)

5. What was the Pharisee's reaction to the scene? What was his main complaint?

_____

_____

_____

_____

Day 2

1. Read Luke 7:40–43. In Jesus' parable of the prodigal son, the older son represents the "secretive" type of sinner—the one who follows the rules but harbors hatred in his heart. How does Luke let us know Simon is this type of person?

Jesus answered and said to him, "Simon, I have something to say to you." So he said, "Teacher, say it." (Luke 7:40)

_____

_____

_____

_____

_____

2. Jesus often had strong words to say against the Jewish religious elite, but here he had accepted an invitation from a Pharisee. What does this reveal about His feelings toward them? Why would He have attended this banquet?

_____

_____

_____

_____

_____

_____

_____

3. In what ways was Jesus' presence at the Pharisee's house similar to the father's attempts to show grace to his older son?

There was a certain creditor who had two debtors. One owed five hundred denarii, and the other fifty. And when they had nothing with which to repay, he freely forgave them both. Tell Me, therefore, which of them will love him more? (Luke 7:41–42)

_____

_____

_____

4. How did Jesus respond to Simon's critical thoughts?

_____

_____

_____

_____

5. What is the point of Jesus' parable about the two debtors? How did Simon respond?

Simon answered and said, "I suppose the one whom he forgave more." (Luke 7:43)

_____

_____

_____

_____

Day 3

[Jesus] turned to the woman and said to Simon, "Do you see this woman? I entered your house; you gave Me no water for My feet, but she has washed My feet with her tears and wiped them with the hair of her head. You gave Me no kiss, but this woman has not ceased to kiss My feet since the time I came in. You did not anoint My head with oil, but this woman has anointed My feet with fragrant oil. Therefore I say to you, her sins, which are many, are forgiven, for she loved much. But to whom little is forgiven, the same loves little."
(Luke 7:44–47)

1. Read Luke 7:44–50. In Jesus' parable of the prodigal son, the father represents God. How does Luke let us know Jesus is acting in that role in this scene?

2. What is Jesus saying to Simon by contrasting the sinful woman's acts of devotion with his lack of courtesy as a host?

3. In the culture of the day, to not wash a guest's feet was tantamount to an insult. What does this tell us about Simon's attitude toward Jesus?

Those who sat at the table with Him began to say to themselves, "Who is this who even forgives sins?" Then He said to the woman, "Your faith has saved you. Go in peace." (Luke 7:49–50)

4. What did Jesus mean when He said, "Her sins, which are many, are forgiven, for she loved much" (verse 47)? What is the basis of her forgiveness (see verse 50)?

5. Why was Simon unable to comprehend Jesus' actions toward this woman? Why was he—like the older son—unable to give or receive grace?

Day 4

1. Read Luke 15:8–10. In this parable, the mention of the woman's "ten silver coins" implies it was all the money she had. How would that motivate her search?

_____

_____

_____

_____

What woman, having ten silver coins, if she loses one coin, does not light a lamp, sweep the house, and search carefully until she finds it? (Luke 15:8)

2. What did the woman do when she found the lost coin?

_____

_____

_____

And when she has found it, she calls her friends and neighbors together, saying, "Rejoice with me, for I have found the piece which I lost!" (Luke 15:9)

3. In what ways is this parable similar to the one Jesus told about the prodigal son?

_____

_____

_____

4. What do both parables tell us about how God views lost sinners? To what lengths will He go to bring all sinners to Himself?

_____

_____

_____

_____

5. Jesus says "there is joy in the presence of the angels of God over one sinner who repents" (verse 10). How should this motivate us to seek out the lost?

_____

_____

_____

_____

I say to you, there is joy in the presence of the angels of God over one sinner who repents. (Luke 15:10)

Day 5

1. Read Matthew 26:57–68. To what lengths did the chief priests, elders, and council go to convict Jesus? What motivated their desire to have Him put to death?

_____

_____

_____

The chief priests, the elders, and all the council sought false testimony against Jesus to put Him to death. (Matthew 26:59)

2. Read John 2:19–21. How did the false witnesses seek to distort Jesus' words so a charge could be made against Him?

_____

_____

_____

_____

3. Read Psalm 110:1 and Daniel 7:13. What was Jesus implying when He said, "You will see the Son of Man sitting at the right hand of the Power, and coming on the clouds of heaven" (Matthew 26:64)?

_____

_____

_____

_____

4. Why did Caiaphas view this as blasphemy? How did he and the council react?

_____

_____

_____

5. The parable of the prodigal son ends with the father telling his older son to rejoice that his younger brother has returned and to join in the celebration. However, Luke records no response from the older son. How does this scene ultimately reveal what the Jewish religious elite's answer was to the heavenly Father's offer?

_____

_____

_____

_____

Prayer for the Week

Heavenly Father, thank You for seeking us when we, like the prodigal son, go astray and rebel against Your Word. Thank You for loving us enough to not only forgive our sins when we repent but also to bring us back into Your glorious presence. Help us to likewise seek out the "worst of sinners" among us so we can faithfully share Your message of reconciliation. We also pray that You will expose any areas of pride or self-righteousness in our hearts. Bring to light any place in which we are just "going through the motions," serving You out of duty instead of love. Help us to recognize our need for grace, accept that grace, and extend that grace to others. In our Lord Jesus' name. Amen. ✳

LEADER'S NOTES

Thank you for your willingness to lead a group through this study of *Parables*. The rewards of leading are different from the rewards of participating, and we hope you find your own walk with Jesus deepened by this experience. In many ways, your group meeting will be structured like other Bible studies in which you've participated. You will want to open in prayer, for example, and ask people to silence their phones. You may want to plan time at the end of your meeting to pray for prayer requests from the group. But the core of the meeting will be your discussion of the Bible study questions.

Each of the questions in the main sections assume the participants have read the relevant chapter from *Parables*. The chapter in the book offers extensive cultural background to the passages to be studied, and that information often isn't repeated in this workbook. If some group members don't have time to read the chapter, you can have someone who has read it summarize information that is relevant to the questions. This summary will probably fit best before you discuss the Bible passages under the "Make the Connection" section.

Ideally, group members will answer all twenty-three of the discussion questions before the group meets. As the leader, you should definitely answer the questions on your own before the meeting. As you do so, put a star by those that you think will make the most effective group discussion. If your time to discuss the Bible study is sixty minutes or less, you may not have time to discuss every question. As long as your discussion is fruitful, it's not necessary to cover every one.

Have a volunteer read aloud the excerpts from the book and the Bible passages before you discuss the questions that apply to them. Also, when you've asked a question, don't be afraid to let people sit in silence. People are often quiet when they are pulling together their ideas, and silence is often a sign they are thinking through them. Avoid the temptation to answer the question yourself, as this will train the group members not to answer for themselves. Instead, wait. Let the question hang in the air until someone shares. You can then say, "Thank you. What about others? Did anyone have a different idea?"

In some of the questions, the participants are asked to share their own experience or consider how the passage applies to them. These are often the most interesting questions to discuss. Encourage as many people as possible to reply to them, but do allow people to pass if they prefer. They may have personal applications that they don't wish to talk about. Avoid going around the circle and having each person respond to questions. Your goal is a conversation that flows as naturally as possible.

Note that the questions under the "Reflect and Respond" section are optional. The intent of these is simply to provide participants with a guide for spending time in God's Word for five days of the coming week. Point out these questions to the group, but know it is not necessary to discuss answers to them, unless someone has a particular insight they want to share the following week. ✳

Preparation

As the leader, there are a few things you should do to prepare for each meeting:

❋ *Read the chapter of the book that corresponds with the lesson.* This will help you to better know the material so you can guide the group discussions.

❋ *Write down your answers to the study questions.* You can compare them to the suggested answers that follow.

❋ *Pray for your group.* Pray especially that God will guide your group members into a deeper awareness of the kingdom of heaven and a deeper commitment to following Christ as their Lord and Savior.

Below you will find suggested answers for the study questions. Note that in many cases there is no one right answer. Answers will vary for those questions, especially when the group members are sharing their personal experiences.

Lesson 1: One Ominous Day in Galilee

1. Jesus's teaching style is to quote an Old Testament passage from the law of Moses and deepen it with His own interpretation and alteration. His teaching is straightforward as He asserts His authority to update the law and tell people how to live.

2. Jesus reads a passage from the prophets and asserts straightforwardly that He is its fulfillment. He then goes on to address his audience's resistance with straightforward language. He refers to the biblical stories of other prophets, Elijah and Elisha, and He uses figurative language, but He doesn't tell stories.

3. Jesus has stopped quoting the Old Testament. His teaching about his kingdom is now couched in stories. He no longer makes open claims about His own authority.

4. If the Sabbath is made for man, then one would look for ways of keeping a day of rest that rejuvenate the body and spirit, rather than ways that simply restrict normal life. The Sabbath would be a celebration, not just a duty.

5. The Sabbath is part of the Ten Commandments. God commanded it, and only the divine Son of God has the authority to declare what is

lawful on the Sabbath or even suspend the rule altogether for some good purpose. People who say Jesus never claimed to be God have to reckon with passages like this one where He claims God's authority.

6. Answers will vary. Some Christians today are caught up in legalism, while others tend to follow our culture's inclination to put one's own desires ahead of any authority—even God's.

7. One reason is because the Holy Spirit was empowering Jesus to cast out demons. In addition, the Pharisees *knew* the Holy Spirit had to be the source of the power, yet they attributed it to Satan. It was their deliberate, knowing lie that made it an unforgivable blasphemy. If they had merely been in error, they could have been forgiven.

8. Merely disbelieving in Jesus is not blasphemous, nor is merely disagreeing with Christians. A person would have to know that the power of God has been at work and yet lie and attribute the event to Satan.

9. The Pharisees were motivated by pride and the desire for power. While people today might not be guilty of blasphemy against the Holy Spirit, they can certainly be guilty of pride and the desire for power.

10. The time for Jesus' crucifixion was still years in the future. He needed more time with His disciples to train them in the ways of God's kingdom.

11. Contrary to what the people of that time expected, Israel's Messiah did not arrive on the scene as a military conqueror or powerful political figure. Instead of rejecting and discarding the outcasts, Israel's Messiah embraced them, taught them, healed them, mended them, and ministered to them. Even the Gentiles would learn to trust in Him.

12. Jesus still embraces, teaches, heals, and ministers to the outcasts. His eyes are on those on the margins of society, not primarily on those who are successful in the world's eyes. That's good news to us if we are on the margins. It's also a call to us to minister to those on the margins in His name.

13. The Pharisees were "rotten trees" that could only bring forth rotten fruit. Their hearts were evil, so they brought forth evil words from their hearts. This inevitability didn't excuse their behavior; it explained their guilt.

14. Answers will vary. Some examples would include a good tree (person) bringing forth true words and honorable actions, recognizing the Holy Spirit in action, and celebrating the goodness of God. Such a

person would adjust his or her own preconceptions about what God would do on the Sabbath in light of this evidence.

15. Answers will vary. For example, someone may note that his or her many words are generally kind, but they reveal anxiety and a strong desire for attention that might need to be moderated out of consideration for others.

16. The Sabbath was supposed to be a weekly reminder of the grace of God, which always stands in stark contrast to human work. It was meant to give people a break from the drudgery of work and give them a foretaste of heaven, when they would enter fully into God's rest.

17. Answers will vary. Some group members will greatly identify with the idea that sin has made work a never-ending drudgery, while others will be grateful they find a creative outlet in their work, or a chance to do something God wants done in the world.

18. Answers will vary. Some group members may be so busy that they find it hard to set aside time to let their minds and bodies rest. Rest is different from noisy entertainment. It allows the body and mind to relax and make space for God. A good rhythm isn't one-size-fits-all, but there's a reason why God set aside one day in seven.

19. First of all, it's a rare individual who can get through life without ever acting out of malice toward someone. But even if we grant the theoretical existence of such a person—whose only sins have been unintentionally harming others and omitting to love his or her neighbor with truly sacrificial zeal—those are still real sins. The most charitable unbeliever still lives in rebellion against God, even if he or she is unusually noble toward fellow humans. It's this rebellion against God that merits eternal punishment, because God really does deserve absolute love and allegiance.

20. Answers will vary. Jesus says even these sins are forgivable to someone who repents and believes. Our resistance may stem from our inability to imagine someone committing truly heinous sins and then truly repenting of them.

21. Answers will vary. Allow some time of silence for group members to think about this question and answer it in their hearts.

22. Answers will vary.

23. Answers will vary. It's not necessary for group members to come up with an action plan that would be mere striving and busy work, but

hopefully something in the lesson has touched their hearts and they want to hang onto it.

Lesson 2: A Lesson About Receiving the Word

1. In the Bible, the *heart* is the core of a person, the executive center. The heart has thoughts and intentions (see Hebrews 4:12). A person thinks with his or her heart (see Proverb 23:7). A person also feels and chooses with the heart and relates to God with the heart. Thus, to be hard-hearted is not just to be emotionally impassive but also to be resistant to the things of God.

2. As we saw in lesson 1, words and actions flow from our hearts. Without external force, it's not possible for us to consistently change our behavior apart from changing the heart. And God isn't interested in forcing us to behave well independent of what we truly think and desire. Jesus said in Matthew 12:33–35, "Either make the tree good and its fruit good, or else make the tree bad and its fruit bad; for a tree is known by its fruit. Brood of vipers! How can you, being evil, speak good things? For out of the abundance of the heart the mouth speaks. A good man out of the good treasure of his heart brings forth good things, and an evil man out of the evil treasure brings forth evil things."

3. The different responses people make to God aren't caused by different genetics—the issue is spiritual. Each of us starts out equally sinful and in need of grace. This means that we are all equally responsible for the responses our hearts make to God.

4. Suffering raises the question as to how a "good God could allow this to happen." A faithful person will remain convinced that God is good even when bad things occur. Such a person will continue to worship God, will pray for the strength to endure, and will seek the prayers of others. The person may question and wrestle with God, but he or she won't abandon God. A person whose faith isn't genuine will go beyond wrestling to outright bitterness toward God and toward his or her situation. This person will conclude that no good God exists.

5. Someone might maintain the pretense of belief in God in order to be well-thought-of by certain Christians. Perhaps he or she wants to date a Christian believer. Or perhaps the person enjoys the emotional high of a certain kind of worship service.

6. Some people have stronger emotional responses than others, and they are naturally more demonstrative than more introverted people.

Such a person may have a habit of responding with enthusiastic emotions to one pursuit after the next, and Christianity may be just the flavor of the month for such a person. On the other hand, sometimes an emotional response to the gospel does go with genuine faith, so we shouldn't necessarily be skeptical of emotional people.

7. When we are preoccupied with things, they become more important to us than the things of God. We devote so much time to making and spending money that we don't have enough time for serving God. The values of the world are our real priorities, and faith gets little time and not much energy. When that happens, our fruitfulness for God's kingdom shrivels.

8. One way to know is to look at the way we spend our time and the way we spend our money. Do we make time for prayer and service? Do we devote a generous portion of our income to God's work?

9. Answers will vary. Examples include, "might makes right," "look out for yourself first," "we each create our own reality," and "if it feels right to you, it *is* right for you."

10. A person's response to the Word of God is dependent not on the one who shares the message of the gospel with him or her, but on the condition of that person's heart. Furthermore, *fruit* is the only evidence that one has heard the Word rightly.

11. Answers will vary. Most of us have felt such a pull at some time, and some of us will struggle against that pull to a significant degree.

12. Like David, who prayed, "Create in me a clean heart, O God, and renew a steadfast spirit within me" (Psalm 51:10), we must approach God with trust and submission, persistently asking and allowing Him to do the necessary work in our hearts that we cannot do ourselves. We must actively cultivate what He is working into us by exposing ourselves to Scripture, prayer, worship, and any other means God wants to use to soften and prepare our hearts.

13. We admit it when we don't understand what Jesus is saying, and we actively pursue understanding. Once we do understand, we put into practice what we have learned and bear fruit.

14. The mysteries of the kingdom are the truths of the gospel that only God knew up until the time Jesus became a man. They include the secret that the eternal Son of God was going to take on human flesh and enter the world as a Messiah very different from the warlike Messiah the Jews were expecting. The mysteries of the kingdom also

include the secret that the Messiah was going to allow Himself to be arrested and crucified in order to bear the sins of the world and that He was going to rise from the dead.

15. Whoever has a partially softened heart and wants to be softened more will find God giving him or her a softer heart and greater understanding of the gospel. But whoever has a hardened heart toward God will find that even his or her glimmerings of understanding of the gospel will be taken away, and it will all seem meaningless.

16. This is hard for people to talk about, so it may be most effective to have people say the fruit they see in other group members' lives. But it's important for people to think about this and to examine their own lives from time to time.

17. Answers will vary. Talk also about the ways you can address those barriers to fruitfulness, such as scheduling time for God as a firm appointment in your calendars.

18. Answers will vary. Most groups have both types of people—the self-critical and the not very self-critical. It's good for people to recognize what type they are so they know what areas in their lives God may be asking them to examine.

19. Answers will vary. It's helpful to persistently pray for a tender and receptive heart, to check in with God regularly throughout the day, to cultivate times of quietness in a busy day, and to stop and become aware again of the Spirit's presence. It's also helpful to cultivate humility and remind ourselves we can do nothing of value without God's help.

20. Reminding ourselves of these things fosters the kind of humility that makes us more willing to yield to the Spirit's work.

21. Answers will vary. These times often involve some degree of suffering or at least discomfort, and we're often unaware at the time that God is working in us. Remembering those times can make us more willing to endure seasons of suffering, because we know that God is at work.

22. Answers will vary.

23. Answers will vary.

Lesson 3: A Lesson About the Cost of Discipleship

1. The *kingdom* is the realm where Jesus is the undisputed king. It is the realm where what He wills is done without resistance. It is that realm where Christ graciously rules over and eternally blesses willing, loving subjects who gladly embrace Him as Lord by faith. Most of the universe gladly does God's will; it is only on our planet that people resist Him. We believers are part of His kingdom.

2. There are many privileges we receive when we belong to God's kingdom. We have eternal life, which we will spend in God's presence. We've begun that eternal life already, and we have His Holy Spirit dwelling inside us, enabling us to do what we couldn't do on our own. We have forgiveness of our sins.

3. If we acknowledge Christ as our Lord, we are committed to doing what He says in the Scriptures. We are committed to making Him our top priority, ahead of all selfish endeavors. None of us does that perfectly, but it is the standard we're committed to move toward.

4. Being "poor in spirit" means to be spiritually bankrupt and have no assets that could earn God's favor. Those who *know* they are spiritually bankrupt know their true condition and are therefore humble before God.

5. In order for us to enter the kingdom of God, a price had to be paid for our sins. The punishment for sin is death, and Christ paid that death penalty with His own life. He took our place in the punishment so we would be cleansed enough to enter the kingdom with His righteousness imputed to us.

6. All human life—all human blood—is precious in God's eyes. But an ordinary human's blood isn't precious enough to pay even for his own sins. Even our dying wouldn't pay the price for our own entry into the kingdom. And the death of one ordinary human certainly couldn't begin to pay for the sins of all of humanity. Christ's blood is so much more precious because He is God in human flesh. He is the infinite one, the sinless one, incalculably above any one of us in value. His blood is precious beyond our imagination.

7. Obviously, it cost Christ the pain of crucifixion and death. But even more than that, it cost Him the unimaginable humbling and limitation of becoming human and living on earth for more than thirty years. We often underestimate the sheer cost of the incarnation. Further, Jesus paid the heavy cost of bearing all our sins and

being separated from His Father while He did so. His cost was far higher than what an ordinary human would pay by dying.

8. We get freedom from eternal punishment. When we think about how bad eternal punishment would be, we see what a valuable treasure we have been given. We also get eternal intimacy with God. God is the most beautiful and most joy-inspiring Person in existence. Eternal intimacy with Him is of far more value than eternal intimacy with our human loved ones—and we get that too if our loved ones are believers.

9. Answers will vary. It's worthwhile to think about what we're withholding from God. Would we say no if He wanted us to suffer a disability in this life? Would we say no if He wanted us to face persecution or humiliation for His sake? Do we expect a comfortable life in this world in addition to eternal life? This week's parables challenge us to ask ourselves if there is any place we draw the line with God.

10. A man found something so valuable that he sold everything he owned in order to get it. He was so overjoyed, so overwhelmed by the value of his discovery, that he was eager to surrender everything he had in order to gain that treasure. That's how valuable the kingdom of God is, and we should be willing to give up everything for the surpassing value of being citizens of that kingdom.

11. Like the hidden treasure, the pearl is worth everything. The kingdom of God is worth whatever it costs us to serve Christ. The difference is that in the story of the treasure, the man comes on it by accident, while in the story of the pearl, the merchant is seeking a treasure. Some of us are like the first man—we weren't seeking the things of God when He revealed the truth about Christ to us. Others of us are like the merchant—we were seeking truth when we found our way to the gospel.

12. Such a person is willing to pay a price for being a citizen of the kingdom. He or she is willing to spend time and money serving God, willing to endure rejection from people who don't believe in God, and humbled by the magnitude of the gift God has given.

13. Jesus is saying it's important to count the cost of an endeavor at the beginning to be sure one is able to pay the cost.

14. Jesus says, "If anyone comes to Me and does not hate his father and mother, wife and children, brothers and sisters, yes, and his own life also, he cannot be My disciple" (Luke 14:26). Jesus means that commitment to Him will have to come before commitment to family. He talks about carrying a cross to the place of execution—being willing to die for Him—and about forsaking all that we have if necessary.

15. At various times in history, God's people have had to pay the steep price described in this passage. Few of us in our society have faced the choice of sacrificing our family or our own lives for the sake of Christ. However, it's important to think about this cost before the situation presents itself.

16. Answers will vary. Most of us have paid some price in terms of time and energy. Some have endured rejection from family or others. Of most encouragement to a small group will be those who have paid a steeper price, such as walking away from worldly success in order to serve Christ. It's not necessary to boast about these costs, but it builds one another up to share them.

17. Joy can be a boisterous emotion or a quiet one, depending on our personality. But there's something missing if we just feel flat when we contemplate the benefits we have received. Sometimes we get so used to having those things that they don't register with us as anything to get excited about. But they are too good to take for granted.

18. Some in your group may be facing decisions about ministry or other sacrifices in God's service. Let your group be a sounding board as they wrestle with a decision.

19. Some group members may find that experience perplexing, frustrating, or even angering. It's not helpful to be angry at unbelievers for not understanding the value of the kingdom, but it is good to acknowledge our anger if it's there. Then we can move past it to godly sorrow and loving outreach.

20. Answers will vary. These are good stories to share with one another in your group.

21. Answers will vary. If names are shared in the group, be sure to pray together for these people.

22. Answers will vary.

23. Answers will vary.

Lesson 4: A Lesson About Justice and Grace

1. We tend to minimize our sins and measure them by our peers rather than by the love and holiness we were born to live by. "Ordinary" sins almost invariably include deceit and malice. None of us makes only well-intentioned mistakes. We fall far short of the love of God and

neighbor that is God's standard. We ignore God. We are indifferent to the needs of others, looking after ourselves above all. Apart from Christ, we are rebels against God's rightful kingship. If we saw ourselves as God sees us apart from Christ, we would see how much we deserve exclusion from God's presence.

2. God's grace is not unjust because Jesus paid the just penalty for our sins. Only the divine Son of God could pay the death penalty for millions of people.

3. If we're honest, we may admit to feeling there are people in society who have committed such heinous acts that God shouldn't forgive them based on belated remorse. But if God wants to bring such a person to repentance, He gets to do so.

4. In most human interactions, fairness is a good standard to use. Even children naturally understand that in a rational world, the rules are clear, the consequences are clear, and everybody gets what they deserve. The standard of fairness appeals to our logical minds.

5. We would all die immediately and suffer eternal punishment for our sins. "For the wages of sin is death" (Romans 6:23).

6. Jesus deliberately makes His landowner outrageously generous. The man pays a more-than-fair wage to those who work all day and is outrageously generous to those hired later. It would be hard to run a vineyard that way and still make money. The story is deliberately shocking to make a point. On the other hand, in relationships generosity is often a better standard than fairness. Parents, for example, need to discipline their children, but sometimes they discern a situation where wiping out the debt is appropriate for a particular child in a particular situation. And marriages work better when each spouse aims to be generous rather than keeping track of what the other person has "earned" through behavior. Still, Jesus is primarily intending to show how God does what a normal businessperson wouldn't do.

7. Those who come to faith late in life and contribute relatively little to the kingdom of God during their time on earth are "the last." As this parable shows, they will receive exactly the same eternal life and intimacy with God as those who have lived their lives as abundantly fruitful believers.

8. Our primary motivation for serving God in this life is love. If we don't care to serve God, we can legitimately question whether we truly love God. If we love Him, then His pleasure is incentive enough. However, there is some indication that as believers we will

be rewarded for our service and that those rewards will be part of what we offer to God in heavenly worship. (See 1 Corinthians 3:12–15 and Revelation 4:9–11.)

9. God is more interested in generosity than in fairness. His grace and mercy overflow in abundance.

10. They are paid on the basis of the landowner's generosity, not on the basis of what they have earned.

11. The early-morning workers thought the landowner's system was based on *earning*, so they felt they should get more than those who worked only one hour. They assumed that if the landowner was going to be extravagantly generous to the latecomers, they should have earned proportionate extravagance. When this didn't prove to be the case, they were no longer satisfied with the more-than-fair wage they received.

12. Answers will vary. Hopefully, the group members recognize the gift they have been given in salvation and are glad for all to receive an equal reward. But if someone admits to feeling a twinge of unfairness when the notorious sinner is saved, you can praise his or her honesty. It's good to get these feelings out into the open and not hide them.

13. Peter thinks that those who have served Jesus the longest and hardest deserve the greatest rewards. He thinks he and his fellow disciples are earning good places in the kingdom. He thinks the whole thing works on the basis of merit—getting rewarded for good work based on how good one's work is.

14. In the parable, Jesus says that everyone who is called to work in the vineyard gets an equal wage. So Peter and the Twelve are not *earning* their places on the thrones judging the tribes of Israel. Their places, and everyone's place, are a gift from God.

15. Answers will vary. Hopefully, the group members will respond to this story with gratitude and be thankful they are not expected to earn places in the kingdom by the extravagance of what they've given up. They should be willing to make sacrifices and do God's work in the world, but not in order to earn their places in the kingdom. We, like Peter, need to get past thinking in terms of earning rewards.

16. Answers will vary. Encourage people to briefly share how they came to faith and emphasize God's initiative. Even for those who actively sought the truth, God was working in the background to draw them with that hunger implanted in their hearts.

17. God wants to call people through us. If we falter in our obedience, He will find another way, but that isn't an excuse for us to be lazy or fearful. God has sovereignly chosen to do much of His work in this world through human agents. We have the privilege of being His partners in the spreading of the gospel.

18. The fact that a person's response to the gospel is ultimately up to God takes the pressure off of us. If we do our best, that's the extent of our responsibility. Also, we don't know if the seeds we plant may bear fruit at some future time. Our job is to be faithful, and the success is up to God.

19. Answers will vary. Some in your group may have been raised in Christian homes and not remember a point in time when God called them. Ask them to talk about their awareness of neediness—or not—during their adolescence or young adulthood.

20. Answers will vary. We are always poor and needy before God, but if we have been walking with the Lord for some time, we may be struck more by the amount of healing we have experienced and the level of security and confidence we now have with God. That doesn't necessarily indicate false pride has taken over.

21. We can't always tell by other people's behavior, but often we can have some sense of another person's possible receptiveness to the gospel based on whether or not he or she seems aware of any need. Those who don't seem to have their lives perfectly together are often the ones who might respond to the gospel if it is offered with humility and friendship.

22. Answers will vary.

23. Answers will vary.

Lesson 5: A Lesson About Neighborly Love

1. A straightforward answer from Jesus would have been, "Believe in Me. Believe that I am the Messiah and Son of God, and put your faith in Me as your Savior and Lord." As Jesus said in John 5:24, "He who hears My word and believes in Him who sent Me has everlasting life, and shall not come into judgment, but has passed from death into life."

2. Our eternal destiny is riding on the answer to this question. All other questions might make our current lives in the world more pleasant,

but this question pertains to our deepest need not only for this life but also for the rest of eternity.

3. The lawyer wasn't seeking a straight answer to a straight question. He wasn't seeking to be informed. He was testing Jesus by trying to start an argument that would prove Jesus to be a false prophet or something else negative. He was trying to embroil Jesus in a debate about the law. Jesus didn't deal with a "test" the same way He would have dealt with an honest question from a genuine seeker.

4. The lawyer should have been convicted by how far short he fell in loving God and his neighbor. He should have been willing to admit that he didn't love even his Jewish neighbors as he loved himself. And he should have known that he needed God's forgiveness for falling short.

5. Many people want to look good in their own eyes and other people's eyes. They have such illegitimate pride that they can't bear to look small in anyone's eyes. Other people have opinions that play a huge role in their sense of who they are. Losing face feels like annihilation to them.

6. The legal expert thought God's righteousness came from keeping God's law, as interpreted by his fellow scholars in religious law. He didn't understand that God's true standard in the law was beyond him and that he needed righteousness to be imputed to him by a perfect sacrifice on his behalf.

7. Most likely you will get some stories of people doing something and some stories of people doing nothing. If group members mention giving money, you can draw attention to the fact that giving money, while laudable, falls short of the total personal involvement the Samaritan showed.

8. Reasons for not taking action include busyness, not wanting to give money to someone who is going to spend it on alcohol or drugs, or not thinking the person deserved help. Compassion fatigue sets in when we are so overwhelmed with the news of poverty and disaster all over the world that we feel we can accomplish little. All of these are explanations for inaction, but they don't *justify* inaction. Instead of acting like the lawyer, who tried to justify himself by redefining the word *neighbor*, we should simply face the fact that our reasons aren't good excuses. We fall short of God's law. That admission is what Jesus wants us to get to as we contemplate this parable.

9. Compassion fatigue is one of the biggest obstacles. It's easier to be compassionate to those we know personally, yet the news media inundate us with needs all around the world every day. Another big obstacle is sheer selfishness—wanting to spend our resources on ourselves and those we care about.

10. Jesus deftly gets out of a technical debate by reframing the question. He points out the important question is not *who we are obligated to care for* but *what behavior qualifies as true neighborliness.* The lawyer might have been able to keep the command if he set the bar of "who is my neighbor" low enough. But Jesus' story says that's the wrong way of approaching it. The command sets an infinitely higher bar.

11. The standard is the Samaritan's behavior. He sacrifices considerable time and resources helping a stranger in need. Moreover, that stranger is a member of an enemy group. This is a rare level of compassion—truly treating a stranger as he would treat himself.

12. A good response is to look for opportunities to be sacrificially compassionate. But it is also a good response to fall at Jesus' feet and say, "I can never live up to that standard! How can I attain God's forgiveness for my failure?"

13. Much like the parable of the good Samaritan, this passage sets the standard of loving our enemies and doing good to those who hate us. We are to behave far less self-interestedly than ordinary people do.

14. Jesus seriously does want us to try to love and do good to those who hate us. And He also wants us to be supremely grateful for the grace of forgiveness when we fall short of this standard of being perfect as God is perfect.

15. Answers will vary. Some in the group may have tried to love an enemy and found it to be a superior way to live. It may even have led to some degree of improved relationship with that enemy. Others may have tried to love their enemies and had only mixed success. All can be grateful for the grace of forgiveness, because surely no one in the group has managed to do this with the consistency of God's standard of perfection.

16. Answers will vary. For some, the fact the Samaritan got involved with a stranger at all will be most surprising. Others may be most surprised by the blank check the Samaritan wrote for the fees associated with the man's care.

17. Answers will vary. Jesus really does want us to grow in our love of neighbors, so seeking opportunities to do this is a worthwhile endeavor. Our salvation doesn't depend on this, but extending ourselves to others is a way of expressing our gratitude to God.

18. Most likely, group members will be acutely aware that their compassion has fallen far short of God's standard and they are in no position to be proud of what they've done. Those who have been compassionate are likely to be particularly humble and grateful for the opportunity to serve.

19. Answers will vary. This is a chance for group members to share stories not just of their salvation but also of anytime God has stepped in and cared for them when they were in need.

20. Answers will vary. We don't earn God's love by our generous responses, but real faith does lead to action of some kind. "But someone will say, 'You have faith, and I have works.' Show me your faith without your works, and I will show you my faith by my works" (James 2:18).

21. Answers will vary. This is a chance for group members to examine their hearts and see if they take grace for granted. It's easy for us to fall into this pattern, but we should be endlessly awestruck by God's forgiveness. God doesn't want us to wallow in guilt, but He does want us to be moved to an ongoing stance of humility.

22. Answers will vary.

23. Answers will vary.

Lesson 6: A Lesson About Justification by Faith

1. God's own righteousness is flawlessly perfect, and to lower that standard even slightly in order to accommodate our sin would make Him unholy. He literally can't be close to people who fall short of holiness because they would be destroyed by that contact. The book of Numbers has stories of mass deaths when the people fall into sin while God is dwelling in their midst. These stories illustrate the incompatability of a holy God and tainted humans.

2. Answers will vary. Some group members will be familiar with the idea of God's standard of holiness, while others will have trouble taking it in. God loves us and understands what we're like, so it may seem that He could have a more "reasonable" standard. Good human parents don't expect perfection from their children, so some may wonder why

God does. But the issue isn't what God expects. He knows we're going to fall short. He's under no illusions. The issue is what is necessary to be in the presence of a holy God.

3. The Pharisees thought God was concerned with outward actions, but Jesus said our attitudes and desires must also conform perfectly to the requirements of the law. A lustful look violates the same moral principle as an act of adultery (see Matthew 5:27–28). To be angry without cause, to insult someone, or to hate another person is to breach the same commandment that forbids us to commit murder (see verses 21–22).

4. *Imputed* means credited or attributed to someone. In the context of the gospel, it means to regard the qualities of one person as belonging to another person. So, we say that Jesus' perfect righteousness is *imputed* or credited to us. It didn't belong to us, but now it is regarded as belonging to us, because Jesus paid the price for our sin.

5. No, God's unearned grace is what enables Jesus' righteousness to be imputed to us. Faith in Christ is the action by which we accept this offer of grace. However, faith isn't mere intellectual assent to an idea; it is faith in a Person, which includes surrender to that Person as Lord and Savior.

6. *Atonement* is reconciliation and restitution (making amends by paying). Jesus paid the price of our sins in order to reconcile us to God. We couldn't atone for our own sins because the price was too high: the death penalty.

7. At the temple, the priests offered animal sacrifices daily for the sins of the Jewish people. Once a year, on the Day of Atonement, the high priest offered a special sacrifice for the people's sins. The Pharisee's tithes covered his part of the cost of these sacrifices. So, the Pharisee assumed the sacrifices covered his unintentional failures to keep the law, and his excellent track record of trying hard to keep the law fulfilled God's expectations of him. He was doing his best, and he believed the temple sacrifices took care of however he fell short. That's how it worked in his mind.

8. Sometimes, people who believe the good they do outweighs the bad do not believe there is a God or a heaven, and they are just living as basically moral people because they were raised to be that way. They believe they will stop existing when they die. Sometimes such people do believe in heaven, and they think they will go there when they die. Or they believe in reincarnation, and they expect to come back in their next life with a reward for how they have conducted themselves

in this life. None of these people expect eternal suffering when they die. They either reject the Christian idea of hell as barbaric, or they think it doesn't apply to them.

9. The tax collector's misery was a sign of his genuine repentance, and this led to his justification.

10. The Pharisee stands and prays "with himself"—to himself. He asks God for nothing. His whole prayer is one long self-congratulation. He congratulates himself for being better than the worst members of society and for keeping the tiny details of his tradition's interpretation of the law. He is unaware that he should be asking for mercy because of his pride and lack of love for others.

11. The tax collector stands far from the holiest part of the temple. He keeps his eyes lowered, for he knows he isn't worthy to even raise his eyes to heaven. He beats his breast as a sign of grief about his sin. His words are an admission of guilt. He calls himself a sinner. He begs for mercy.

12. The tax collector goes away justified not because he has quit his corrupt job and changed his behavior but because he has begged for mercy, believing that he needs it and that God is a God of mercy. He doesn't know that Jesus will die for him, but he's looking to God for atonement rather than to himself. He has faith in God as the One who provides atonement.

13. The phrase "He has borne our griefs and carried our sorrows" implies that Jesus carried what was rightfully ours—our sorrows that result from sin. "He was wounded for our transgressions" states the price he paid for our sin. "The chastisement for our peace was upon Him" refers to the punishment he took that we deserved so we could have peace with God. "The Lord has laid on Him the iniquity of us all" also conveys this idea of Jesus carrying our sin. Finally, "By His knowledge My righteous Servant shall justify many, for He shall bear their iniquities," shows that by bearing our sins Jesus justified us. He had us declared righteous in God's eyes.

14. God wasn't improvising and going to Plan B (the cross) when Plan A (the law) failed. Rather, He was unfolding a carefully laid plan that He wanted His people to understand when it was fulfilled. Even when He gave the law, He already knew His people would break it. He knew the system of temple sacrifices wouldn't be enough to compensate for their sin. He knew the Son of God would have to become man and suffer.

15. This part of the passage predicts Jesus' resurrection. He died as an offering for sin, but He didn't stay dead. He rose to life, which is how He could then see His "seed" (spiritual offspring) and prolong His days.

16. Professing Christians can usually spot outright idolatry. They're not going to bow to a statue of a Hindu god or dabble in spiritism. However, they can easily slide into the belief that they can follow the external practices of Christianity well enough to keep God happy without examining their hearts for sins such as greed, deceit, malice, and indifference to their neighbors. Pride at one's religious observance is a real snare for people who are basically "good."

17. Answers will vary. Those who haven't been tempted in this way may be able to point to good teaching they received that has inoculated them against the allure of rule-keeping.

18. Repentance is impossible without humility because we have to humble ourselves in order to admit our sin. If our hearts are filled with pride, we refuse to admit we have a problem. However, if we have humility, there's a chance we will confess the problem. With pride, it is infinitely harder.

19. Answers will vary. Some of us find justification by faith alone to be a great relief, while others feel embarrassed there is nothing we can do to save ourselves.

20. A truly penitent tax collector would stop his extortionate practices or leave the business altogether. This action doesn't earn his justification, but it would be the natural outcome of genuine repentance. A saved tax collector is one who wants of his or her own accord to bear fruit in keeping with repentance. In John 8, after Jesus refused to condemn the woman caught in adultery, He told her, "Go and sin no more" (verse 11). Jesus wasn't saying salvation came through works but was encouraging her to follow the natural response of a heart that had been forgiven. Likewise, the tax collector didn't have to clean up his business practices in order to be forgiven, but if he was truly penitent, he would want to do so.

21. Answers will vary. Most of us know at least one notorious sinner who seems unlikely to come to grips with his or her sin. But God often delights in drawing such people to Himself. This question is intended to motivate group members to pray and even reach out in friendship to someone who needs Christ.

22. Answers will vary.

23. Answers will vary.

Lesson 7: A Lesson About Faithfulness

1. People could have a lot of power over their future if they knew when the Lord was returning. For instance, if they knew He was coming back within their lifetimes, they might not have to plan for money and healthcare in their elder years. If they knew He was coming three centuries from now, they could plan their concern for evangelism and their care for the planet with that timeframe in mind. They would feel they had so much more control just knowing. Control is the main reason people want to know.

2. God wants us to live as if He were coming back at any moment but still be prudent in planning for the future as if He were going to wait another several centuries. He wants us to be consistently faithful every day, both for the short term and the long term.

3. Answers will vary. A surprising number of people are drawn into expecting the Lord's return within a few years. It relieves them of the pressure of long-term planning and often motivates them to evangelism and self-sacrifice for others. However, these are things we should practice even if the Lord won't return during our lifetimes.

4. In Ephesians 5:15–20, Paul urges us to live wisely and make the most of every opportunity to further God's kingdom agenda. He exhorts us to know and do the Lord's will, to avoid drunkenness and debauchery, and to be filled with God's Spirit. He speaks of worship-filled talk, singing God's praises, and making thankfulness a habit. These are just a few of the practices of one who is watchful for the Lord's return.

5. Paul tells his readers to expect the Lord to come suddenly and to prepare for it by living as "sons of the day" (1 Thessalonians 5:5). He contrasts children of the night, who get drunk and misbehave, with children of the day, who stay sober and keep watch. He speaks of wearing faith, love, and hope of salvation as armor. Faith, love, and hope are three crucial virtues that we need to make habitual as we prepare for the Lord's return.

6. Being watchful means living in a godly and sober manner. It means, "Denying ungodliness and worldly lusts, we should live soberly, righteously, and godly in the present age, looking for the blessed hope and glorious appearing of our great God and Savior Jesus Christ" (Titus 2:12–13).

7. In this world we are often judged by results rather than faithful effort, but in God's economy the results are up to Him. God knows He has

given different resources to different people, and He doesn't want us to worry about results. Instead, He wants us to concern ourselves with doing as much as we can with what we have been uniquely given. This relieves us of a huge potential burden of worry.

8. We don't know what service in heaven will be like, but we do know it will involve work that will invigorate us rather than exhaust us. We might make music and art as worship. We might cultivate gardens. We might organize group endeavors.

9. Our work matters to God. It's not something that gets in the way of our real lives; we can serve God by doing work that He wants done in the world. If we're involved in a service that makes people's lives better, or we help to get food from farm to table, we are doing something that contributes to God's kingdom. There will always be frustrating aspects of work in this world, but if we treat it as something God has entrusted to us, we can use it for His glory. As Paul wrote, "Whatever you do, work at it with all your heart, as working for the Lord, not for human masters, since you know that you will receive an inheritance from the Lord as a reward. It is the Lord Christ you are serving" (Colossians 3:23–24 NIV).

10. The evil servant's error is believing that his master is delaying his return. This leads him to live as if his master were never coming back. He acts as if he will never be held accountable for his actions.

11. The foolish virgins' error is in believing the bridegroom will not delay his coming. This leads them to fail to plan for the long term by not bringing extra oil for their lamps. Their error is in a way the opposite of the evil servant's error, but it leads in a similar way to a failure of faithfulness.

12. Answers will vary. This is partly a temperament issue: some people are more naturally wired to live for the moment and not think much about the future, while others are more naturally inclined to be future thinkers. The problem with living only in the moment is that it can cause us not to make long-term plans that could advance God's kingdom. The problem with not living as if Jesus will return soon is that it causes us to become complacent and not sense the urgency of sharing the gospel.

13. The talents represent the resources and abilities God has entrusted to each of us for use in serving Him in His kingdom agenda.

14. The unprofitable servant was wicked and lazy. He wasn't really afraid of his master; instead, he just couldn't be bothered with investing

his talent in order to bring a return. If he had truly feared his master, he would have made the effort to do at least something profitable with the silver.

15. As we are waiting for the Lord's return, we must be diligent in investing the resources God has given us for His kingdom. We must not be preoccupied with self-serving pursuits, for we will have to give an account for what has been entrusted to us.

16. Answers will vary. We need to be like the wise servant who did his job and cared for others at all times. In this way, we will be ready to face the Lord at any moment and say that our lives were consistent with our faith in Him.

17. Answers will vary. Some possibilities might include planning for one's elder years, investing in our children and grandchildren, and caring for the earth's resources. We should carry on activities such as these in a manner that reflects the fact we will one day have to give an account of our faithfulness to God. We don't know the Lord will tarry another thousand years; we only know that He might.

18. Answers will vary. Group members who can't see their own assets may benefit if others in the group suggest abilities and strengths they see in them. Sometimes we see others' gifts more clearly than we see our own.

19. Answers will vary. Note that sometimes, what seems mundane in our lives looks like evidence of faith in other people's lives. Maybe they are diligent parents. Maybe they are faithful to their spouses. Maybe they are conscientious at work. Or maybe they have tasks at church that they carry out week after week.

20. Answers will vary and parallel the answers given for question 19. Faithfulness is often "unspectacular."

21. The previous question referred to what we are *already* doing, while this question asks what we *could* do. The goal is not to pile burdens on people, but to dream big. We must look for the opportunities that might be hiding in plain sight.

22. Answers will vary.

23. Answers will vary.

Lesson 8: A Lesson About Serpentine Wisdom

1. A love of money can conflict with righteousness and godliness if our desire to keep what we have motivates us to go against God's will. If we're trusting money to take care of us, we aren't trusting God to take care of us, which weakens our faith. If we're investing our time in accumulating and spending money, we have less time to invest in acts of love and generosity to others. Gentleness is a non-retaliatory way of responding to someone who does something that harms us. The love of money undermines gentleness by inflating our pride and making us prone to anger when our money is threatened.

2. Material wealth can disappear in a bad economy or be stolen. It's unreliable as a locus of ultimate value. More important, as we accumulate material wealth, our hearts get attached to it. The biggest risk of accumulating wealth is that it can draw us away from desiring God and depending on Him for our needs.

3. This is a difficult question. In Jesus' day, people didn't "retire" because most didn't live long past the age when they could make a living. Today we have the possibility of living for decades with physical or mental limitations of aging that make work difficult. So we have to plan for that possibility. Likewise, college is a feature of our world that has no adequate first-century parallel. Perhaps the best way to bridge the gap between Jesus' teaching and our modern context is to build practices of generosity into our budgets along with saving for the future. Both need to be priorities. But if we can't afford both, generosity needs to takes precedence. It's hard to see how Jesus would approve of our spending years in idleness, seeking entertainment and personal fulfillment, when we could be working and giving to others.

4. For the "sons of this world," all they have to look forward to is an early future. They can see the results of planning in other people's lives, so it's vivid in their minds what will happen if they set goals for retirement or they don't. They are 100 percent certain that they will have to deal with those future years unless they die unexpectedly. There's no doubt in their minds that old age is real.

5. If the analogy with the "sons of this world" holds true, the failure on the part of the "sons of light" to be equally diligent in investing in eternal things could be caused by them not being completely certain that eternal life is real. They've never seen people enjoying eternal rewards or suffering eternal punishment, so to them it might seem less vivid than this world. Another reason could be that they're convinced eternity is real but they're vague on how to invest in it. They don't know that caring for the needy among God's people and

JOHN MacARTHUR | PARABLES WORKBOOK

investing in the spread of the gospel are things that will win them eternal friendships. They figure they are saved without doing those things, and that's the priority. Everything else is vague or secondary.

6. Laying up treasures in heaven means doing things that have eternal value, such as spreading the message of the gospel or giving money to those who do. It also means treating God as our life's highest value, because He is the greatest treasure in heaven. Treating God as our life's highest value has implications for the way we spend our time and energy as well as our money.

7. If we spend money on helping the needy among God's people, we will gain their friendship and God's friendship in eternity. If we spend money on the spread of the gospel, we will gain the friendship of those who come to Christ as a result.

8. We naturally tend to treat money as a resource to be used for our own good. Many times, we treat money as a resource to be used for our families' good, and only when our families' needs are taken care of do we start to think about other people. We need to make a mental shift to see other believers and potential believers as part of our true family. Money is a resource to be used for our true family's good, and our true family includes all those who could be touched by the ministry of the gospel.

9. Answers will vary. The goal here is to get group members to let the idea take root so that it becomes a motivating factor in their lives. It should trigger emotions like joy.

10. The steward demonstrated his shrewdness in that when he found out he was losing his job, he cheated his master in a way that would make his master's debtors owe him patronage. He was assuring he would have well-placed friends who would support him when he was unemployed. He thought ahead and planned for his future cleverly, with a good understanding of the way the system worked in his culture.

11. The parable is shocking because Jesus seems to be commending a completely unscrupulous, dishonest, and selfish person.

12. Jesus wanted to get His disciples' attention with a story that would stick in their minds and needle them in the future when they made decisions about money. He wanted this story to be unforgettable to them. He also wanted to pique their curiosity so they would pay attention to the explanation of the parable that He was about to give.

13. Our acts of generosity toward our brothers and sisters in need, and our generosity toward the ministry of the gospel, demonstrate our trustworthiness with the resources that God has entrusted to us.

14. God is the true owner of everything we possess. There is truly nothing in this life that we "possess," for we all are caretakers and managers of God's property.

15. Serving money means to treat money as our highest value. If accumulating money to spend on ourselves and our families is more important to us than spending money on God's agenda, then we are serving money ahead of God. Or, perhaps we are serving our families ahead of God. Certainly we have responsibilities to our families, but we need to discern where we draw the line between money for family and money for the needs of those outside our families. Ultimately, if we are serving "mammon" (worldly wealth) we aren't truly Christians, because no one can have more than one master—and God is the Master of true believers.

16. Shrewdness is simply cleverness in understanding how the world works and living accordingly. The issue is how the world actually works and what is really in our best interests. If this life is all there is, then our best interests will motivate us to pursue things that will lead to our own material gain. However, if this life isn't all there is, then our best interests will be to pursue things of eternal value.

17. One example would be cheating at work if we're confident we won't get caught. This could be considered shrewd if there were no God, but extremely unwise if there is a God who sees and judges all things. Becoming a person who cheats and pursues worldly gain will make us unfit for the work God has for us to do in His service.

18. Investing in spreading the gospel is shrewd if God is real but a complete waste of resources if God is not real. This is why we need to be convinced of what is real. If we refuse to spend our time and money on God's agenda, it suggests we don't actually believe God is as real as the material world around us.

19. Hopefully, by now group members are taking serious stock of their spending habits and realizing that the work of God needs to be an important line item.

20. We are continually bombarded with messages that this world is all there is and that true happiness lies in accumulating possessions and pleasures in this life. These messages insist that we need what

the world has to offer. In order to believe and act on what God says, we have to stand against all of those messages.

21. The immense value of investing in eternity is that it is what will truly last. Material wealth is temporary and can disappear in a blink of an eye. Our worldly status and success is fleeting. Our friends on earth come and go. However, the investments we make in eternity will endure. We need to see that eternity is what really matters. It's not vague but real and concrete—more real, in fact, than our temporary world.

22. Answers will vary.

23. Answers will vary.

Lesson 9: A Lesson About Heaven and Hell

1. When most people think of Jesus, they consider His gentleness and His endless compassion for sinners. They assume this means He never talked about anybody—especially ordinary people—suffering eternal punishment.

2. Jesus certainly had a tough side to His character. He didn't take delight in sending people to hell, but He wasn't soft on sin. He longed for people to repent and escape hell, yet He was realistic that many wouldn't heed His call to repent. He was under no illusions about human nature and spoke about hell precisely to motivate people into taking the danger seriously and paying the price of repentance.

3. Jesus told a crowd who asked this question, "This is the work of God, that you believe in Him whom He sent" (John 6:29). Calling Jesus "Lord" is easy but insufficient. Truly putting our whole faith in His atoning sacrifice and abandoning all self-directed religious programs is what Jesus requires us to do.

4. Answers will vary. If group members realize their church rarely teaches about the reality of hell, they can assess whether they think that's a problem. Jesus' teaching on hell is an important part of the gospel, for there are real consequences for rejecting Christ. Everyone in a church needs to be fully aware of those consequences.

5. The importance of teaching people about the horrors of hell is important for the same reasons as teaching children about the dangers of touching a hot stove—the peril is real, and we don't want them to be burned through ignorance. One reason some people say they believe in God but don't practice an active faith is because they don't

think there are any negative consequences for doing so. If they can manage this life on their own, and they expect the next life to be good regardless of whether they lead a life that is faithful to the gospel, they assume a life of faithfulness is unnecessary. They desperately need to know their prospects after death are dismal if they don't get serious about putting their true faith in Christ.

6. Answers will vary. Group members can assess whether they are among those who find hell an embarrassment, an inconvenience, an irritant, or an offense. The idea of hell ought to be troubling for us, and we should be genuinely uncomfortable at the thought that our unbelieving neighbors are destined for hell—even though they may be kinder or more likeable than many Christians we know.

7. We need to understand that hell is a place of serious and eternal suffering. We need to be afraid of hell—afraid to go there ourselves and unwilling to let anyone we care about go there if we can prevent it by sharing the gospel. We need to not soften hell to make it more "acceptable" but hate the idea that anyone ever goes there. This is motivation for us to share the gospel message.

8. Some people can't imagine that a merciful God would inflict everlasting suffering. Surely, they reason, He will end it with the annihilation of the damned. *Eternal* suffering seems like cruel and unusual punishment for those whose unbelief in this life spans only a few decades. But the Scriptures say otherwise. Humans are eternal beings, and our fates for good or ill will be eternal.

9. Answers will vary. Some will be motivated to share the gospel with loved ones. Others will accept the teaching dispassionately. Others will be uncomfortable with the teaching and have trouble believing this is the destiny facing the unbelievers they care about. Jesus' teaching on hell should motivate us to do some soul-searching and compel us to share the gospel, not push us away from God. It's important for us to understand that God doesn't enjoy the eternal suffering of the damned. He gives them the destiny that unbelief merits, but He takes no pleasure in doing so.

10. This parable shows that hell is a place where the unrepentant suffer eternal punishment. Once someone is in hell, he or she has no longer any opportunity to repent and go to heaven. People feel everlasting regret, anguish, and longing in hell, but they don't repent and change their hearts—the rich man still sees Lazarus as a nobody who can be sent on errands to help him. In hell there is no possibility of escape and no rest. Not one fingertip's drop of relief will ever ease the suffering or diminish the pain.

11. Jesus is saying that hell is real and is full of people who didn't expect to be there. He is also saying that Scripture ("Moses and the prophets") is sufficient to powerfully provide all the information people need to know why and how to repent of their sins and cast themselves on the mercy of God through Christ.

12. Once people are in hell, it will be too late to ask for mercy. Their characters are fixed and are incapable of repenting. They have become, for eternity, the sum of the choices they made in this life.

13. Some who saw Lazarus's resurrection decided to believe in Jesus. Others went to report the incident to the Pharisees. The chief priests and the leading Pharisees discussed the incident, and for them it was the last straw that ended their hesitation to kill Jesus. Far from convincing them to believe in Him, it convinced them that He had to be stopped by any available means.

14. The Pharisees had already made up their minds about Jesus because He didn't follow their interpretations of the law of Moses. When He did something miraculous, they assumed He was a false prophet empowered by Satan to do those miracles. They had completely closed their minds to the possibility that He was empowered by the Holy Spirit.

15. The chief priests and Pharisees didn't accurately understand and believe Moses and the prophets (the Old Testament Scriptures), so they didn't believe in Jesus even when He raised a man from the dead.

16. Answers will vary. Many unbelievers have no firsthand experience with the Bible, so they have either no opinions about it or have negative opinions based on what they have heard that it says.

17. Usually, the message about sin and damnation is not the most effective place to start with an unbeliever. We interest someone in the Bible as a trustworthy resource when we link it to a need the person has, such as questions about how to be a more effective parent or how to handle money. Sharing a parable about money can be intriguing to someone who has no background in the Bible. From there, we can invite them to explore the fascinating character of Jesus in one of the Gospels. They can discover for themselves Jesus' love, wisdom, and uncompromising stance on eternal destiny.

18. Answers will vary. Most Christians, if they stop and think about it, will realize the Word of God has played a decisive role for them. That should motivate them to trust the Word when it comes to the needs of their unbelieving neighbors.

19. "Weeping and gnashing of teeth" conveys feelings of deep but fruitless sorrow and regret, anger and frustration, and perhaps self-pity.

20. Darkness conveys the utter absence of the light of God, of truth, and of beauty. Light is associated with goodness and darkness with evil and the desire to hide (see John 3:19–21). Those who have chosen hell have chosen to be distant from God, so they have chosen the darkness of His absence.

21. Answers will vary. It's natural to be frightened and repelled by images of hell. Hopefully, the terrifying aspects will motivate group members to repent of their own sins, be grateful for Christ's atoning sacrifice, and reach out to the unbelievers around them.

22. Answers will vary.

23. Answers will vary.

Lesson 10: A Lesson About Persistence in Prayer

1. We can be tempted to "lose heart" if we pray again and again for the same thing but don't see any evidence that our prayers have been answered. In such situations, we might conclude that God isn't listening to us or doesn't care. In the case of praying for the Second Coming, the answer might not even come during our lifetime.

2. As in the days of Noah, the wickedness of man today is great in the earth. For many people, every intent of their hearts is evil continually. There is great violence on our planet, with people using weapons more powerful than ever before in history.

3. Answers will vary. Some group members will be deeply aware of wars around the world, or dysfunctional politics, or corruption in business, or laws and customs of society that run counter to God's ways. Some will gain hope from conversions or acts of brave faith.

4. The assurance of God's promises in Scripture can give us courage as we go to the Lord in prayer. The memory of God's faithfulness in the past—during our own lifetime as well as generations of believers back as far as the times depicted in Scripture—can also give us encouragement and support.

5. Many of us are perhaps hindered in our prayers due to low-intensity unbelief. We feel that our prayers haven't been answered yet, and this prevents us from expecting what we perceive to be the answer in the future.

6. Contact with fellow Christians who are bold in prayer can be a big help, as can praying with others in a group or having a regular prayer partner. Keeping a list of prayer requests and answered prayers can help us be persistent and recognize all the times that God has intervened in the situation.

7. There is so much harm done in the world today by callous people that we easily become discouraged in our walk with God if we are not grounded in the knowledge that the day is coming when those wrongs will be righted. The Second Coming of Jesus gives us the strength to keep doing what is right even when most people around us are doing wrong. Knowing the end of the story gives us confidence and stability.

8. Answers will vary. Some group members probably won't know they were supposed to be praying for the Second Coming. They may see it as something that God will do in His own time but isn't for them to ask for explicitly. Other group members will have a passion for Christ's return that drives them to pray for it.

9. Answers will vary. Instead of making group members feel fruitlessly guilty for not thinking much about Christ's return, talk about how they can integrate real passion for Christ's return into the responsibilities they have in the world. How can they tell the difference between responsibility and worldly distraction?

10. God is profoundly different from the judge. The judge cared nothing for God's laws or human need, but God cares deeply about His own laws and about our needs. He cares about widows and other vulnerable people. He cares about justice.

11. The parable argues from the lesser to the greater. If even this worthless, diabolical reprobate of a judge will give justice to a persistent pleader, then surely the utterly just and merciful God will do so.

12. God will avenge the elect when Christ returns to judge the wicked. This may not occur in our lifetime—the wicked of our day may live full lives and have gone to hell long since. This may not seem like speedy justice, but in God's eyes it is. We may not witness those who martyr Christians being punished in this life, so we have to be patient and know that one day those individuals will face God's judgment.

13. The Second Coming will be sudden like lightning, but more important, it will be brilliantly visible like lightning in a dark sky. There won't be any need to ask, "Is that really Him?" Christ's first coming was humble, and He deliberately left it open to debate whether He

was the Messiah or not. His Second Coming will not leave any room for such questions. He will come dramatically and openly as King and Judge.

14. In the days of Noah and Lot, God's judgment came on the people with only the warning given to those who acknowledged the Lord. For those who rejected God, the judgment came on an unexpected day when they were busy with their normal lives. Only those who knew God were warned and prepared to escape the judgment. We who love God already have our warning of the Second Coming. Christ will come on that day as Judge without any further notification about date and time. He will come when the world is busy about its normal business and paying no attention to God.

15. This passage makes it clear that in the parable Jesus isn't primarily talking about prayer for our personal needs, though we should certainly pray persistently for those needs as well. He wants us to pray for His return to bring justice to the earth. We live in a world that is full of evil, as in the days of Noah and Lot, but God will one day bring justice. We should pray earnestly for that day of justice to come.

16. Answers will vary. Some will be deeply moved with joy, while others will find the details overwhelming.

17. God is committed to minimizing the suffering of His church. Certainly, around the world today Christians are dying for their faith or losing their homes and becoming refugees. For them, it's likely hard to imagine a worse tribulation than what they are going through. But the Scriptures assure us this suffering has limits, and the worst outpouring of God's wrath will be withheld until His people are safe with Him.

18. The good news is that Christ is returning to bring justice to the world and that believers who are alive now won't have to go through that terrible time. In addition, God will allow multiple opportunities for people to repent before they suffer His wrath. In the end, God and good always win.

19. The delay builds faith and perseverance in us, which are valuable virtues. We don't think of God as our sugar daddy or vending machine, who exists to grant us our every whim. We don't become spoiled and selfish. We gain humility.

20. Answers will vary. If group members are shy about telling their personal needs, model openness by sharing one of your own long-running prayer requests.

21. Answers will vary. Hopefully, group members will say they have the strength of character and faith to persevere even if they never see the answers to their deepest prayers during their lifetime.

22. Answers will vary.

23. Answers will vary.

Bonus Lesson: A Lesson About God's Love

1. The younger son's attitude toward an inheritance was inappropriate because he had no gratitude for the legacy his predecessors had passed down to his father and, by extension, to him. This was especially inappropriate in Jewish culture because the passage of family estates from father to son was governed by the law of Moses.

2. The prodigal son quickly discovered that "all that glitters is not gold." The road he chose in pursuit of worldly pleasure turned out to be a path to destruction. He realized this when his money ran out, his "friends" abandoned him, and he was so hungry that he was forced not only into feeding pigs but also desiring the food they were eating.

3. Paul tells us that before we met Christ, we were "aliens," "strangers from the covenants of promise," and that we had "no hope." We were just like the prodigal son who had scorned the rich inheritance his father had provided.

4. Jesus' listeners would have been shocked that the father freely offered forgiveness to his son at the first sign of repentance. In the culture of that time, to save face the father would have been expected to put together a formal employment arrangement.

5. The father's actions reveal that he had been diligently and persistently waiting for his son's return. Not once had his intense love for his son wavered during the young man's rebellion against him. This shows us that God is eagerly waiting for the first sign of repentance in a sinner. When He sees this, He runs to embrace that sinner and welcome him or her home.

6. The father ran not only because he was overjoyed at the son's return but also because he was anticipating the contempt of the village that was sure to be poured out on him. The father ran in order to be the first to meet his son and deflect the abuse. Likewise, our heavenly Father runs to us, forgives us, removes our shame, and restores us.

7. The elder brother embodies the main lesson because Jesus was directing the parable at the attitudes of the Pharisees. The older brother represented the Pharisees in Jesus' day, and today he depicts all those who trust in their own self-righteousness for salvation.

8. It is clear the elder son resented his father because he had no respect for him and no interest in doing the things that pleased his father. He pretended to be a good and loyal son, but his lack of concern for his younger brother shows his inability to extend mercy as his father had done. The fact that he was out in the field and unaware of the celebration is a depiction of how far removed he was from his father.

9. Both the younger and older son harbored an attitude of hostility and rebellion toward their father. They both wanted what they considered to be rightfully theirs, on their own terms, so they could live how they pleased. The older son just went about it differently—by waiting for his father to die.

10. The younger son was driven by a desire to live the way he wanted to live on his own terms. He did not want to live under his father's rules, so he rejected his father's care to pursue what he thought would be the good life. Likewise, people today reject God because they want to lead their lives on their own terms, without His "rules." In doing so they deceive themselves and end up destitute like the prodigal son.

11. The young man came to his senses when he realized he was starving while many of his father's hired servants had food to spare. His plan for reconciliation involved persuading his father to hire him as one of those servants.

12. The father's plan for reconciliation was to forgive his son completely and without any requirements for service. The father's plan was different because he loved his son and was eagerly waiting to extend grace and mercy to him.

13. The older son was not aware of the celebration because he was out in the fields. This tells us that he routinely distanced himself from his father.

14. The father extended grace to his eldest son by going out to find him, just as he had done with the prodigal son, and inviting him to join the celebration. He was seeking to show his love and bring reconciliation.

15. The older brother was angry because he felt his years of service had earned a higher position for him in his father's house than his younger brother, who had openly rebelled and squandered the inheritance he

had been given. His own self-righteousness and attitude that "service brings salvation" make him unable to extend grace to others.

16. The prodigal son's open rebellion led him to a place where he recognized his mistakes and his need for his father. For the older son, this revelation didn't come because his attitude that he was doing "good enough" in his father's eyes had blinded him to the fact he was just as distant from his father.

17. When we are distant from our heavenly Father, we do not concern ourselves with the things that concern Him. This can take the form of apathy toward unbelievers, failure to extend grace to others, jealousy for the blessings others receive, and a judgmental attitude to those who are "greater sinners" than ourselves.

18. It is human nature to judge people based on outward appearance. We have to be close to God and know His heart to be able to see people the way He sees them.

19. The older son, like the Pharisees, was not willing to hear the word and understand it, and as a result his life did not bear fruit for God's kingdom.

20. Jesus promises in Revelation 3:20 that when we hear His voice and open the door to our hearts, accepting His call as our Lord and Savior, He will enter in and be with us. God is always seeking to close the gap that separates us from Him.

21. John says that when we answer our heavenly Father's urgent call and experience His love, it compels us to show that same love to others. "We love Him because He first loved us" (1 John 4:19). If we truly love God, we will want to serve as His ambassadors to the world, urgently calling unbelievers to experience His grace, mercy, and salvation.

22. Answers will vary.

23. Answers will vary.